The

National 3 Peaks

- Taking Up The Challenge

with

Steve Williams

DISCOVERY WALKING GUIDES LTD

The National 3 Peaks - Taking Up The Challenge

Second Edition - February 2012
Copyright © 2012

Published by
Discovery Walking Guides Ltd
10 Tennyson Close, Northampton NN5 7HJ,
England

Mapping supplied by **Global Mapping Limited**
(www.globalmapping.com)

[Mapping sourced from Ordnance Survey] This product includes mapping data licensed from **Ordnance Survey®** with the permission of the Controller of Her Majesty's Stationery Office. © Crown Copyright 2005. All rights reserved.
Licence Number 40044851

Photographs
All photographs in this book were taken by the author Steve Williams, Alec Thompson, Mark Gibson, Geoff Cowing or Dave Robinson, with the exception of those of the Crown Hotel, Penyghent, Whernside and Ingleborough which were provided by Fotocraft Images*

ISBN 9781904946816

The National 3 Peaks
- Taking Up The Challenge

CONTENTS

Steve Williams was born in South Shields, Tyneside in 1955. When he was eleven years old, he and his family moved to Scotland which was where he met the Thompson family. The youngest son, Alec, became a lifelong friend and fell-walking companion.

At sixteen Steve took up cycle touring and explored most of the UK. However, for the past three decades Steve's abiding passion has been mountain walking in Britain. During this time he and Alec have walked most of Britain's long distance paths and have become thoroughly familiar with the Cumbrian mountains, the Pennines, Snowdonia and the Western Highlands of Scotland. His proudest achievements are cycling from Land's End to John O' Groats and walking the Pennine Way…oh, and now, successfully completing the National Three Peaks in under 24 hours.

Residing these days in Oxfordshire - which unfortunately is bereft of mountains - with his wife Chris and young daughter Nicole, Steve runs his own management consultancy and training business. Educated in Scotland and Oxford, Steve holds two masters degrees in business disciplines.

In his professional life, he has travelled extensively and to many unusual locations, but is most at home when walking the Lake District fells.

This is his first book.

Mark Gibson

First and foremost, thanks go to Geoff Cowing and Mark Gibson for providing impeccable support and safe but speedy transport during the challenge itself, and for somehow maintaining their good humour throughout. We truly were one team of four, and I believe Geoff and Mark took pride in our achievement too, as they should, because we could not have done it without them.

Geoff Cowing

Thanks to Alec Thompson for ..... just about everything, but mainly for a good laugh, before, during and afterwards. I hope we tackle many more challenges together in the future.

Alec Thompson

The Team

Thanks are also due to my wife Chris and Alec's wife Ve for their forbearance throughout and assistance with the pre-challenge preparations, as well as to Sue Cowing who kept the North East contingent of our team on track, and to my young daughter Nicole whose enthusiasm was really encouraging.

Feedback, encouragement and advice on the writing of this account were gratefully received from David Brawn and Brian Rothwell. Richard Griffith, Mike and Karen Chipchase, Brian and Sue Rothwell and my wife Chris kindly undertook the onerous task of proof-reading various drafts. Thank you all.

Permission was generously granted by both Guy Newbold and the Wasdale Mountain Rescue Team to replicate respectively his article and the team's incident report.

Finally, thank you to my friends Alec Thompson, Geoff Cowing and Mark Gibson for contributing photographs. Several other photos were provided by Dave Robinson, and Fotocraft Images (www.fotocraftimages.co.uk).

Undertaking the National Three Peaks walk has become an amazingly popular challenge. It is estimated that over forty thousand people start it each year. By far the biggest proportion of these 'challengers' will take part in a charity organised event aiming to raise money for their favoured cause. Others will be independent teams doing it for the personal challenge. A few may be taking part in corporate team-building events. A certain percentage in all of these categories will be experienced mountain walkers, but most will probably be relatively inexperienced.

It seems that more and more people are seeking personal milestones in their lives; seeking to test themselves, their stamina, their grit and determination. For many, the National Three Peaks provides one such milestone. But it can be even more. It can be great fun, an adventure, a memorable, enjoyable experience of team and individual achievement. For a few it can even be a life-changing event.

Sadly, for others, it can be a failure rather than an achievement; a disappointment rather than a celebration; depressing rather than uplifting. One of the most common reasons for this outcome is preparation - or rather the lack of it - combined with mistaken or unrealistic expectations about the event and perhaps even themselves. To be sure, the Three Peaks Challenge is never going to be a walk in the park. But with proper preparation and know-how, it is attainable for most people. Alec and I did it at the ages of 55 and 51 respectively.

**Mark, Steve, Geoff and Alec
at the foot of Ben Nevis, just minutes before the start.**

That's the reason for this book. When we started to research and plan for the challenge we found quite a lot of information was readily available on routes, timings, advice on training and hillcraft. But nowhere could we find this advice combined with a full account of a successful challenge attempt. What we really wanted and needed was to get a feel for what we would be facing. We wanted to gauge our capabilities against others who had already succeeded. We wanted to identify with their highs and lows and anticipate or forestall our own. So whatever your reasons for taking up the challenge, whatever your level of mountain experience, young, old, or in between, we hope this account is helpful.

So here's our story, plus suggestions on training, walking routes - including GPS Waypoints from the actual paths we walked - driving routes, navigation, equipment, meals, accommodation and lots more besides. Our Challenge Plan ran to 11 pages of text and checklists. It is included at the end of the book for you to copy and amend as you wish. To make it easier to distinguish between the narrative sections and the advisory sections of this account, you will find hints, tips and advice in italics throughout the book.

Arnold Palmer once said,

"The harder I practise, the luckier I get."

So, good luck!

"Great things are done when men and mountains meet. This is not done by jostling in the street."

(William Blake. 18th century poet and painter)

"You know, I've always wanted to watch the sunrise from the top of **Scafell Pike**," said my good friend Alec.

With these words, uttered over a pint one Easter weekend, a series of events was set in motion that ended with us tackling the Three Peaks Challenge some fifteen months later.

Hooked on the idea already, I asked, "What do you mean?"

"I mean bivvying overnight on the top and getting up to see the dawn."

Romantic as this idea might seem in other company, for Alec and I this was really just a plausible idea for another expedition in the Lake District hills. Friends for almost forty years, and now both somewhat overweight and out of condition fifty-somethings, we still walked the hills when we could. A date was set there and then; the night of Monday 26 June.

We planned to meet at **Seathwaite in Borrowdale** at 6.45 p.m. for a 7 p.m. start to allow both of us to do most of a full day's work before travelling to the Lakes, myself from Oxfordshire, Alec from **Dumfries**.

Heavily laden with overnight kit, the climb was steady, the weather fine,

Alec nearing the summit of Scafell Pike

with drifting mist on the tops. We scrambled up alongside **Taylorgill Force**, then joined the path to **Sty Head** and thereafter along the **Corridor Route** to **Lingmell Col**. We arrived at the summit by 11 p.m. with the light almost gone and head torches at the ready.

We made up our beds. There is no vegetation on the top of **Scafell Pike**. It's one of the roughest mountain tops in the district. Everywhere it is either sharp rock or huge boulders, except for one tiny patch of small stones just to the right of the steps to the summit shelter where it is possible for two people, separated by a protruding rock, to lie relatively flat and level.

Having cooked our supper, had a celebratory beer and a whisky night cap, which had admittedly added to the weight of our packs; in the pitch dark at midnight we prepared to crawl into our sleeping bags.

Just then, a trail of head torches appeared in the distance from the **Wasdale** direction, followed in a minute or two by some faint murmuring, puffing and panting. A party of eight youngish guys, perspiring but buoyant, straggled to the top. They seemed as surprised as we were to have company on the summit. It turned out they were 'Three Peakers'. Having started on Snowdon, they had just summitted their second mountain.

"Two hours and on schedule," one of them announced.

Five minutes later, having recruited us as nocturnal photographers in the meantime (rare beasts I'm told), they departed for **Wasdale** and **Ben Nevis**.

We set the alarm for 4 a.m. - sunrise was predicted for 4:35 a.m. This time, as we crawled determinedly into our sleeping bags I said,

"What a bloody cracking challenge. Do you think we'd be up to it?"

"Dunno," was the non-committal response. Within minutes Alec was snoring seismically.

The mist descended and the clouds rose from the valleys. At 4.35 a.m. visibility was approximately 100 metres. No spectacular sunrise, but a seed had been sown…

Two DECISION TIME

The rest of 2006 passed without a lot of joint hill walking activity. The idea though was still lodged in both our minds, it was just dormant. Early in 2007 I decided to revive it.

"So are we going to have a go at these Three Peaks or what?"
"I will if you will" replied Alec.

I suspect this is how many of these 'challenge' expeditions start. Someone speculates that it would be a laugh; a casual 'yes' over a pint and before you know it, you're committed. Mind you, this was something of a repeating pattern for Alec and I. Possibly we have a predilection to impetuosity and a tendency to commit first and worry about the detail afterwards.

At least we weren't complete novices. Many years previously we had walked most of this country's long distance paths, most notably the **Pennine Way**, as well as cycling from **Land's End** to **John O'Groats**. But, it had to be admitted, that was decades ago. And the maximum distance either of us had ever walked in one day - albeit with full packs - was twenty seven miles. As Bill Bryson noted in his book 'A Walk in the Woods', "Distance changes utterly when you take to the world on foot. A mile becomes a long way, two miles literally considerable, ten miles whopping, fifty miles at the limits of conception".

It was now that I broke the news to my wife Chris, who raised her eyebrows and shrugged her shoulders - a familiar combination - said a few encouraging words and prepared herself to be bored constantly by my Three Peaks obsession over the coming months. Until our daughter Nicole was born six years previously, she had been a keen fell-walker herself, so she could identify with the challenge involved. Plus she knew that I always needed a 'project', so she probably thought it was as well this as anything else.

Before anything else, Alec and I needed to know the rules of the game, so I started some research. It seemed there were several different reasons and motivations for people tackling the Three Peaks. At one end of the scale there are numerous charitable bodies that organise mass events to raise funds, with many participants never having set foot on a hill, or maybe even a gentle slope, before. At the other, are the smallish privately organised groups or even individuals who do it for the personal challenge, sometimes sponsored, sometimes not. There are also several firms in the business of guiding parties in their challenge bid. Finally, there are some corporate groups that use the challenge as a team building vehicle.

There is no official National Three Peaks Challenge event (whatever you may read in other publications or websites); rather each charity, team or individual organises their own.

Alec and I clearly fell into the 'independents' category.

The 'real' challenge entails climbing and descending all three mountains within twenty-four hours. The clock starts as you take the first step towards your first summit and ends when the descent of the last mountain is complete. Starting points for each mountain are various, but are either road-heads or car parks at the beginning of established paths. All driving and rest time is included. Having said all this, some charitable bodies and commercially organised events run thirty-six, forty-eight or even seventy-two hour fur-lined luxury events. There is even a forty-eight hour Three Peaks Challenge by public transport. However, for us, the 24-hour test was the motivation, so there was never any consideration given to an extended duration.

Depending upon the routes chosen, the total distance is between 23 and 27 miles/37 - 43.5 kilometres, with 9800ft/2900m of ascent which breaks down as follows:

Ben Nevis (starting at **Achintee**)
        9 miles/14.5 kms, 4370ft/1290m ascent
        Estimated time up: 2hrs 45; down 2hrs 15 (For
        starts at the **Ben Nevis Visitor Centre**, **Glen Nevis**, add ½
        mile and 7 minutes to both ascent and descent.)

Scafell Pike (starting at **Wasdale**)
        5.8 miles/9.3kms, 2900ft/885m ascent
        Estimated time up: 2hrs 10; down 1hr 40

Scafell Pike (starting at **Borrowdale**)
        8.5 miles/13.7kms, 2900ft/885m ascent
        Estimated time up: 2hrs 45; down 1hr 50

Snowdon (starting at **Pen y Pass**)
        8 miles/12.9 kms, 2400ft/730m ascent
        Estimated time up: 2hrs 15; down 1 hr 40

Snowdon (starting at **Pen y Pass**, ending at **Llanberis**)
        9 miles/14.5 kms, 2400ft/730m ascent
        Estimated time up: 2hrs 15; down 2 hrs

Although exacting - because of the timescales involved - there was unlikely to be any real physical danger, in contrast to Bill Bryson's description of the Appalachian Trail, when nearly everyone he talked to, "had a gruesome story involving a guileless acquaintance who had gone off with high hopes and new boots and came stumbling back two days later with a bobcat attached to his head, or dripping blood from an armless sleeve...."

There are no bears, wolves or rattlesnakes on the Three Peaks. Of course the challenge is physical in that you have to be fit enough and fast enough to do the job in the time allowed. It is psychological insofar as it is necessary to stay motivated and to have the resilience to overcome any setbacks. It is also logistical. Poor planning and organisation seems to account for as many failures as exhaustion or injury.

Finally, it's a navigational challenge. The selection of the best routes both for driving and walking is crucial, as is the ability to find them on the ground and stick to them. Stories abound of Three Peakers wandering lost for hours on **Scafell Pike** and such inexperience reportedly accounts for the majority of callouts for the Wasdale Mountain Rescue Team on summer weekends. In June 2007, the following report was filed, and speaks for itself:

*"Wasdale MRT was called to rescue a young male walker who had collapsed on the summit of **Scafell Pike**. He was in a party of three who were doing the Three Peaks Challenge. The three walkers were all in their twenties and from outside the area. One of the party had become separated from the other two whilst he was trying to get help from his mobile phone. He had an altimeter watch therefore no grid reference was available but he could give an elevation. The team searched where the party said they were but did not find anyone. The team then widened the search and at 3.45 a.m. the collapsed walker was found on the **Eskdale** side of the mountain. He was given food and warmed in a bivvy tent and could eventually be walked off the mountain down to **Wasdale Head**. After a further search the third missing walker was located. He was assisted back up to the summit and also walked off the mountain.*

*Whilst searching for the collapsed walker a further group of four walkers were found sheltering in the **Mickledore** stretcher box. They were subsequently reported missing by the police but fortunately the team had already found them and escorted them off the mountain. The team had significant difficulty getting the rescue vehicles back down the valley due to the severe congestion on the road from Three Peaks Challenge vehicles parked up. Twenty team members were involved and the incident was closed at 6.30 a.m."*

We intended to ensure we would not replicate such blunders.

The received wisdom seemed to be that to have a chance of success you needed to complete **Ben Nevis** in under six hours, and **Scafell Pike** and **Snowdon** each in under four hours. This allows ten hours for driving.

No-one really seems to know who first had the idea of stringing the ascent of the three mountains together within a 24-hour period, but its execution would not have been possible before 1972 when Britain's longest motorway, the **M6**, was completed.

Challenge walks have long been a favoured activity amongst outdoor enthusiasts. For many years, the forty mile **Lyke Wake Walk** was the most popular challenge, but over the last decade or so, it has been much overshadowed by the Three Peaks Challenge. And one can understand why. There is a romance attached to climbing the highest mountain in each of the mainland countries that is absent in a 40-mile bog slog across the **North Yorkshire Moors**.

The three mountains are all located close to the western seaboard of Britain. The first recorded ascent of **Snowdon** (1085m 3560ft) was made by botanist Thomas Johnson in 1639.

It was another one hundred and forty two years before another botanist, James Robertson was recorded as the first to summit **Ben Nevis** (1344m 4408ft). Southey, the Lakeland poet, and friend of William Wordsworth made the first recorded climb of **Scafell Pike** (978m 3210ft) in 1802. All three no doubt had been climbed for centuries before by local shepherds or hunters, or even Neolithic man.

The road to Wasdale Head (photo A Thompson)

We fully recognised that the Three Peaks was a challenge to people much younger than ourselves, so before making the final go/no-go decision, we felt we needed to establish the 'training gap'. Consequently we agreed that on 16th February we would tackle **Scafell Pike** from **Wasdale Head** as a test run, giving it everything we'd got. That should give us a good measure, we thought.

The idea was also to test out the route and a few other little techniques. For example, on the real thing, there would be no time for food breaks, so we decided we would eat before we got onto the hill, not on it. All we would carry would be one 'emergency' sandwich plus some nuts and raisins.

The drive around the back of the Lake District from our meeting point at **Penrith** took almost two hours, but by 11 a.m. we were off, leaving from the lane end at **Brackenclose**, next to the **National Trust Campsite**. The

The way up Lingmell Gill to Scafell Pike - in shadow (photo A Thompson)

weather was mild and dry, with cloud down to 600m (2000ft), so pretty good conditions for February.

The path up Brown Tongue

The route initially follows **Lingmell Gill** and then climbs, fairly steeply, over **Brown Tongue** and up to **Hollow Stones**.

Pushing hard up this, with the sweat running into our eyes, we had a choice to make. At the beginning of **Hollow Stones**, the path diverges; right to **Mickledore**, or left to **Lingmell Col**, with this latter alternative being much the better. We went left. On slightly easier ground now we arrived at

the col and then turned right for the final thirty minute pull to the summit.

We did it, exhausted, in 1 hour 50 minutes up - which included a ten minute delay because I carelessly left my map case behind at a drink

The bridge to Brackenclose

The 'Roof' of England. Alec enjoying a well earned rest at the summit shelter on Scafell Pike.

stop - and 1 hour 20 minutes down, with an additional five minutes on the top. A total time of 3 hours 15 minutes was better than we had dared hope for. The decision was 'go'.

Having established that, the aching agony which accompanied our every move for the next three days certainly reinforced our admission that we were out of condition and lacked stamina. We had pushed as hard as we could, even jogging part of the descent and could not have repeated the feat once that same day, let alone twice.

Alec looking north from the summit

We learned other important lessons too, some of which seem really obvious in retrospect.

Drink breaks - and drinking lots and frequently is essential - take a great deal of time, as each walker has to divest himself of his backpack, rummage around for the bottle, take a drink while gasping for breath - and then reverse the process. We agreed to buy platypuses - polythene drinks bladders with drinking tubes - so that we could drink on the move in future.

We had walked with two walking poles each and found these enormously helpful. These became fixtures. They helped to steady us, spread the muscular effort away from just the legs, helped to maintain the forward momentum and reduced the pounding that our knees took on steep descents.

And I decided not to walk with a map in future, but to create route cards that I would be unlikely to put down if we stopped.

There had been little navigation required on this particular day as the path was clear on the ground the whole way. However, we decided we would take joint responsibility for this in future. Whoever was in front, would navigate.

So as we reviewed our performance in the **Wasdale Head Inn** over a well deserved post-walk beer, our minds turned to some of the key preparations we needed to make. We needed a support vehicle, and a driver, ideally two. We had

Wasdale Head Inn

Wasdale Head in December sunshine (photo A Thompson)

to organise equipment and accommodation.

The first of these issues resolved itself that very evening when my brother-in-law Geoff, who lives in **Darlington**, volunteered to drive.

A fan of Emmerdale and Liverpool FC - probably in that order - Geoff is droll, unflappable, laid back (horizontal) but thorough and with an eye for detail. Geoff, it had to be said, had mixed qualifications as a support driver. The fact that he had a new and decent sized car definitely swung it. And we had no other offers. But seriously, I knew that once he made the commitment he'd see it through.

A few weeks later Mark, a friend and work colleague of Geoff's, also volunteered. On this form, it was going to be easy!

Three GETTING FIT

"Training is everything. The peach was once a bitter almond; cauliflower is nothing but cabbage with a college education."

Mark Twain, author

Now our preparations began in earnest. Alec had already been walking a minimum of four miles each day, and I now adopted the same regime. Being self-employed meant that I had the advantage of frequently working from home. On those days I decided to use my lunch break as a training session, eating a sandwich on the move to save time. However, I often also spent days on site with clients, staying away for nights at a time, or having to leave home very early or getting back really late. I imagine that these kinds of challenges to regular training must affect lots of people these days. With some imagination, and a willingness to walk at any hour of the day, in light or dark, I found it was possible nevertheless to train every day. In the four months of preparatory training I missed only five days. The earliest start I made on a training walk was 5 a.m., the latest 10:30 p.m. At weekends we both tried to increase the distance, to six, eight and eventually twelve miles per outing, so that on a weekly basis we were walking thirty to forty miles.

We both decided to lose some weight too. Every extra pound of flesh just increases the burden you have to haul up the hills. By the time we tackled the challenge, I'd lost almost a stone and Alec had lost a stone and a half.

We both trained on metalled roads or paths, in my case in the minor country lanes of West Oxfordshire. After a few initial muscle aches, our fitness levels built surprisingly quickly. Our training walks became increasingly energetic and faster and our typical average walking pace became 4.1mph/6.6kph.

I know that many people training for the Three Peaks do so by climbing mountains. While there is nothing like doing the real thing as part of your preparation, our experience is that even a weekly fellwalk does not maintain fitness; some daily exercise is essential.

Alec was lucky because he had **Criffell** 570m (1867ft) on his doorstep and he used this as an intermittent training outing.

However, we did recognise that we needed to tackle at least a couple of major mountain walks to build and test our stamina.

We mulled over various possibilities, including climbing **Helvellyn** three times in one day. We eventually settled upon the **Yorkshire Three Peaks**, and climbing **Snowdon** twice on the same day. The **Snowdon** outing would serve two purposes; providing exercise, and as an opportunity to try out and become familiar with some alternative ascent routes.

The Crown Hotel, Horton (photo Fotocraft Images)

We set the date for the **Yorkshire Three Peaks** (Y3P) for Wednesday 18th April. I was working in **Leeds** on the 17th, so we decided to stay over at the **Crown Hotel** - actually a pub - in **Horton-in-Ribblesdale** that night and start the walk at first light.

The **Y3P Challenge** entails walking up **Penyghent**, **Whernside** and **Ingleborough** and all the connecting miles between them within a twelve hour period; a circular route of 24 miles with 1800m (5800ft) of ascent. We had climbed all the hills before individually, and had tackled **Penyghent** as part of the **Pennine Way** too, but had never tried all three together.

Alec was already at the pub when I arrived at 5:30 p.m. and put a pint in my hand as I arrived. He had been there since mid-afternoon and by now knew all the incumbent locals, bar staff and the landlady on first name terms. He had also had detailed conversations with other residents who had just done, or were about to do the **Y3P.** One bunch of middle aged guys turned out to have done both the **Y3P** several times as well as the National Three Peaks (N3P). Their assessment was,

"If you can do the **Y3P** in nine hours or under, you'll eat the National Three Peaks."

Given that we were aiming to complete the **Y3P** in ten and a half hours, this was not as reassuring as it was meant to be. We were also somewhat overawed to meet a 63 year old chap who tackled the **Y3P** every year and had just completed it in eight hours and twenty minutes.

That aside, an enjoyable evening was had, with good beer, food and like minded company. We were wise enough to prepare our packs that evening.

This time we were equipped with platypuses (filled with our own isotonic mix of 50/50 fresh orange juice and water, with a pinch of salt), creatine energy tablets and emergency nuts and raisins.

Alec had kindly let me take the only single room with an ensuite bathroom. This probably was as a result of an accident I had had many years previously when the two of us were walking on the **Coast to Coast Long Distance Path**.

We had arrived at **Shap**, booked into our B&B which was a quaint old higgledy-piggledy cottage with sloping floors and squinty walls. We ate, then headed for the pub. It turned into a good night which got even better when at eleven o' clock we got a 'lock in'. At about 2.00 a.m., having drunk just a little more than we should have, we returned to our lodgings by way of several deep puddles and an inconvenient shrub or two. My recollection is hazy but I have no doubt that our attempts to be quiet failed miserably. Alec can't whisper, and I think I knocked a picture off the wall…

Anyway, into bed to sleep it off. Except a couple of hours later I got the urge for a pee. I sleep nude, but all was quiet, so I decided to risk heading down the corridor - in the dark - to the toilet. In my befuddled state, I forgot that the route to the bathroom involved two steps down, two more paces then two steps up, followed by a 90° turn to the left. I missed the first two steps, and with a major crash fell smack into the second two steps onto my ribs. Shocked and in agony I only just resisted the urge to scream, and urgently crawled - I couldn't stand upright - to the bathroom where I lay gasping for breath. Amazingly no-one came to investigate, so once the pain had subsided somewhat, I did what I needed to and crept back to bed. It says something about the soporific and anaesthetic effects of Cumbrian ale that I was able to go back to sleep with what later turned out to be three cracked ribs.

This time Alec was taking no chances...

We planned to rise at 4:30 a.m. and be off by 5.15 a.m. the next day. The landlady at **The Crown** could not have been more helpful, setting out a 'help yourself' breakfast for us so we could leave when we wanted. And thankfully, twenty years on, we repaid her kindness with somewhat more sober behaviour. Perhaps we are growing up, after all…

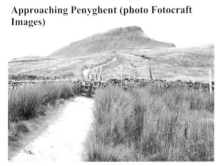

Approaching Penyghent (photo Fotocraft Images)

Our itinerary for the Y3P was first to walk south through **Horton in Ribblesdale**, turn left at the end of the ribbon of village houses and follow the minor road to **Brackenbottom**, where the path up **Penyghent** begins. From there, across country to **Whernside**, then a shorter trek across to **Ingleborough**, followed by a final six mile descent back to **Horton**.

It was still dark as we left the pub at 5.15 a.m., but by the time we arrived at **Brackenbottom** we were walking in the silver pre-dawn half-light. The sky was clear, the air cold and as we ascended **Penyghent**, there was a crisp frost on the ground. As we gained the top after exactly sixty minutes, we were in full sunshine.

The next stretch to **Ribblehead** was very boggy. This was where Alec's clever ruse of staying several lengths behind paid dividends. He was able to steer a much drier course than me, as I repeatedly leapt with extravagant vigour into holes I couldn't even see. It also required some careful navigation.

I had printed off stage by stage directions from www.go4awalk.com and put these back-to-back with the same section of 1:25,000 Ordnance Survey map, then laminated them into a series of 6 route cards. This eliminated the need to carry maps, map case, and guidance notes. The 15 cms x 10 cms route cards were hole-punched in one corner and linked with a treasury tag.

We managed to stay on track and arrived at **Ribblehead**, ten miles in, after three hours.

Whernside from the Y3P track (photo: Fotocraft Images)

At this point Alec announced that he had developed a blister, so he applied a patch of moleskin. Just time for a sandwich and we were off again, in pleasantly warm sunshine. From here onwards, we had no further navigation problems. The path up **Whernside** was not difficult, just something of a grind, and we made the top after 5 hours 1 minute.

For the first time, at the summit we encountered other walkers. We had to remind ourselves that it was only a quarter past ten in the morning. Then it was down to the valley for the next cross-country section, passing the **Old Hill Inn** where we replenished our water supplies, and on up **Ingleborough**. We were getting tired by now, so the ascent was a bit slower, but we still managed to overtake a mountain biker carrying his machine up.

We arrived at the summit within 7 hours 30 minutes. We were well ahead of our target time of ten and a half hours.

After another five minute break we started the last leg. This was an easy, but seemingly never ending descent back over to **Horton**. We pushed on as hard as we could, with Alec limping now from a much enlarged blister.

Ingleborough from Ribblehead (photo: Fotocraft Images)

We completed the circuit at 2.37 p.m.; nine hours twenty two minutes after we started, still full of walking.

This performance boosted our confidence immensely. For the first time we really believed we were capable of completing the National Three Peaks. Even the after-pains weren't so bad this time, and were gone after a couple of days.

In terms of lessons learnt, the platypuses were a boon, but we realised that 1-litre bladders weren't sufficient for long treks and resolved to buy bigger ones.

I had struggled to hold the route cards at the same time as walking with two walking poles, and in future decided to try walking with a small belly bag in which I could secrete them.

The creatine and glucose tablets we had used (made by Lucozade and bought on the internet) worked well for us and we decided to get more for the real thing.

Alec's blister served as a warning. On the actual challenge it could be a disaster. As it was he missed a week's training while it healed. For those who have not come across moleskin before, we can recommend it. It's fabric on one side and completely self-adhesive on the other, so it doesn't slip on the blister. Another great product is the Compeed blister patch. It forms a protective second skin over the blister. Both can be found in good pharmacies in the foot care section.

Finally, the Yorkshire Three Peaks turned out to be an excellent choice as a training event. It closely mirrors the distance involved in the national event, if not the total amount of ascent, and as a result it provides a good measure of the fitness and stamina required for the N3P. More importantly, it is a challenge in its own right and generates the same mix of nervous energy, commitment, and camaraderie. My own conclusion would be that if you can finish the Y3P in ten hours or under, then you are capable of completing the N3P.

After a couple of weeks back in the usual daily training regimen, our next major outing came around. The afternoon before our walk, we met just off the **M6** near **Crewe**, and headed across to **Pen y Pass**. Our road route took us around **Chester** and along the **A55**. This would be the route we would take on the N3P so it was useful to drive it and get a feel for how fast the journey might be and to pinpoint any speed cameras. In the event it was a quick and easy trip, with good signposting. It augured well for the real thing.

Pen y Pass Youth Hostel

We had pre-booked at the **Pen y Pass Youth Hostel**, right opposite the start of the next day's walk. Car parking here is limited, but the hostel has a few allocated bays in the public car park, if you're early enough to get one. That day we got a place but others weren't so lucky. The attendant must have leapt out of bed on the wrong side that morning. We watched him for a good few minutes. With apparent relish he seized the opportunity presented by drop-offs and pick-ups to harangue the unfortunate culprits. My advice is to ignore it, smile, and take your time.

This was the first time either of us had stayed in a hostel for at least a decade, despite being passionate hostellers in our youth, (we had drifted towards camping - better curfew times!). Some things had not changed at all. To borrow a description from Pete McCarthy, author of McCarthy's Bar, ".. the showers still had the residue of other people's second-hand water, with a tide mark of short curly hairs ..". The self-catering kitchen had all the usual hostel accoutrements - including soggy tea towels - and the dormitory still had that whiff of disinfectant, polish and sweaty feet.

But .... there was a TV in the common room, a choice of menu for the evening meal, and my God! A bar serving real alcohol! Always having prided ourselves on our open-mindedness, we tested out these last two innovations and approved. The beer certainly made it easier to humour the school party of teenagers and their teachers.

It was also reassuring that hostels still attract oddballs of all ages. This one had a harmless but seemingly lost and lonely old guy in his seventies and slippers, who by his own account couldn't stay more than one night because, "you'll never get round them all if you hang around". He didn't specify whether he meant all the hostels in Wales, Britain, or the world, but we wished him well.

In a former life this hostel had been the **Gorphwysfa Hotel**. During the Victorian era many mountaineering clubs were formed with regular 'meets' at key locations such as huts, guesthouses and hotels. The **Gorphwysfa** was one such location. George Mallory of Everest fame stayed here with a climbing party in 1913, and the hostel still has the signed guest book on display.

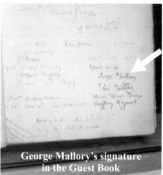
George Mallory's signature in the Guest Book

After dinner we headed down the road to the **Pen y Gwyrd Hotel**, which was, and indeed still is, a renowned climbers' haunt. The last time I'd been here, at Easter 1994, the atmosphere was vibrant and the place was heaving with brawny outdoor types including the women. Unfortunately, tonight we were the only customers. But we'd still recommend a visit. It has a distinct atmosphere.

The most interesting part of the inn is the **Everest Room**. It is set out as an alpine hut; the walls lined in pinewood, it has substantial wooden benches all around the perimeter. The ceiling has been signed by many of the great characters of the mountain and athletics world, including Tensing Norgay, Edmund Hillary, Chris Bonington, Chris Brasher and Roger Bannister amongst others. Growing bored with our own company in such illustrious surroundings, after a pint or two we headed back to the hostel, had a night cap and turned in.

By 7 a.m. the next morning we were on the hill. Our plan for the day was to ascend **Snowdon** using the **Miners' Track**, descend the **Llanberis Path**, then turn around and reverse the route to the summit again. We would then descend for the second and final time, using the **Pyg Track**, which is reputedly named after the initials of the **Pen y Gwyrd Hotel**, but actually is named for the **Bwlch y Moch**, the **Pass of the Pigs** in Welsh.

As well as testing our stamina, this seventeen mile round trip was aimed at familiarising us with all of the path options for the N3P. At this point in time we were favouring ascent by the **Pyg Track** and then down to **Llanberis**. This would enable Geoff and Mark to drop us off at **Pen y Pass** without the need to park, and then to collect us later in **Llanberis**. Ascent

from **Pen y Pass** confers a sizable advantage as the start point is already at 359m (1100ft).

It was a sunny day with a brisk cool breeze; just right. The first three miles of the **Miners' Track** are very easy, a steady incline on a made, gravelly path. The only hiccup came when Alec decided to don his bandana, stopped to do so and then couldn't find it in his pack. His searching took fully five minutes and involved the emptying of at least half its contents. I found this intensely frustrating and an example of unnecessary delays that had to be avoided on the actual challenge.

After passing **Llyn Lydaw** and the upper lake - **Glaslyn** - the **Miners' Track** started to grind upwards, with a stiff climb all the way to the obelisk at the col between **Snowdon** summit and **Carnedd Ugain**.

It was not until we reached the summit after the last fifteen minute pull along the ridge that we met anyone; construction workers labouring on the new mountain-top restaurant that eventually opened in summer 2009. Some of them had obviously just crawled out of their tents, heavily wrapped up and beating their arms against their sides. One started to chat to us and after a few seconds asked,

"Where did you start from?"
With an air of puzzlement Alec replied,
"The bottom."
The worker looked at Alec hard, wondering if his leg was being lifted, but Alec retained his deadpan expression.

"No, what I meant was .. ," but he gave up.
"All the best lads," he finished, giving us undeservedly the benefit of the doubt. It was my favourite moment of the day.

The original summit restaurant, once labelled 'the highest slum in Britain'

by Prince Charles, was built in 1935 and designed by Sir Clough Williams-Ellis who also founded Portmeirion, the weird Italianate village not far from Snowdon, which was used as a film location for the cult TV series 'The Prisoner'.

Hafod Eryi - the new Snowdon Restaurant

At a cost of over £8m, the **Summit Visitor Centre** has its critics. If you're doing the N3P, you won't have time to nip in for a pint or a bite to eat; just as well according to the Telegraph food critic who claimed that **Hafog Eryri (**summer house) ".. must be the world's only £8m restaurant to forget the food. Be that as it may, one has to admit that the new building is starkly impressive".

The gentle breeze at **Pen y Pass** was now a youthful gale, buffeting us violently, so we touched the trig pillar and turned around immediately, this time heading down the **Llanberis Path**. The idea of selecting this route was that on the real thing, it would be a gentle descent and easy underfoot. Neither of these proved to be true, the track being much rougher and steeper in places than I recalled. It also felt a good deal longer than its five map miles. Still we stuck with it and were relieved when we arrived at **Llanberis**, where we turned around and headed back up. This was something I'd never done before and psychologically and physically, I found it a real grind, and so I discovered later did Alec. I felt more dispirited than at any point on the Y3P, yet we had only done nine miles.

Just as we reached **Clogwyn** station Alec announced that he was nursing a

Looking back along the Pyg Track

blister, so gratefully we stopped for him to dress it. We then plugged on to the col. It was a function of how unpleasant we found this second ascent, that we decided not to go all the way to the summit this time but to head down to **Pen y Pass** from the col. We rationalised that for the purposes of a time trial, all we needed to do was add fifteen minutes to our time from the col to **Pen y Pass**.

The **Pyg Track** consisted of a steep zigzag descent, followed by a gently undulating decline for a couple of miles, followed by a final steep descent.

Our ascent time was better than we could have hoped for and our overall time of 3 hours 8 minutes between from **Pen y Pass** to the summit and back was alright. But I was very disappointed that we had managed to save only twenty-two minutes in descent compared to ascent. Actually, this time was our joint time. I had been slightly quicker, but it was still not good. Our performance was poor. We should have been able to shave more time off. I was frustrated, because I had put my all into it.

Double stile at Bwlch y Moch, where the path for Crib Goch joins the Pyg Track

"Are you happy with that then?" asked Alec as he always did after one of our training outings.

"No, we're good going up, but crap coming down. We've got to get quicker. And you've got to practise when you do your **Criffell** walks and speed up your descents. We're letting ourselves down."

This was an honest appraisal and I still feel an accurate one, spoken directly. But it wasn't what Alec wanted to hear after busting a gut on a double ascent of **Snowdon**.

"How the heck do I train for quicker descents?" he asked. I left the question unanswered.

"We're not as young as we were you know." This was all too true. I had knackered knees and he had dodgy hips, but I hated the excuse of advancing years. As ever we went in search of a pint. We found one.

Back we went to our daily training walks. A couple of weeks passed and I phoned Alec to see how things were going. I hadn't heard from him, which was unusual. I soon found out why.

"Hullo," he answered.
"Hi it's me, how are you doing?"
"Alright, training's going okay, but I nearly packed it all in last week."
"What! Why?"
"Well, you obviously don't think I'm fast enough on descents. And I can't get any faster by training harder." Then came the same points he'd made before; knackered hips, advancing years and so on.

"I thought, okay, if you're not happy, stuff you then, you'd better just do it on your own"

He was really pissed off and feeling quite down. This was real alarm time for me. I did not want to do it on my own, although I could have done so. I wanted the spirit and laughs and excitement of a joint enterprise. If that meant being slower, then it was a deal I was willing to make, even though I still disagreed with his premise that training wouldn't improve performance.

"But anyway, I've decided that I'll stick with it," he continued. I breathed a silent and heartfelt sign of relief.
"I really want to do this, and I'm damned if I'm going to miss out on it and spite myself because of this," he finished.

The next few minutes consisted of me eating humble pie and mending bridges, multi-skilled metaphor mixing I know, but that's how it felt. I was conscious of wry looks from my wife Chris, with whom I had shared my frustrations, which said "I told you so, you never learn." Alec and I ended the call completely amicably, laughing and joking in our usual way. But it had been a close call.

I was shocked. It brought it home to me how different character types respond to situations and to direct feedback, even though it had been invited - kind of. If the roles had been reversed and Alec had told me I needed to quicken up, I would certainly have defended my corner immediately, but then I would have pulled out all the stops to do better than him, knackered hips, knees and general decrepitude notwithstanding. He had behaved completely differently, having stewed privately on things for many days, before luckily coming to the decision to continue. Given the kind of work I do, it was a lesson that I should not have had to learn again. Ouch!

The importance of interpersonal and team dynamics are issues that I explore further in Chapter Nine. But for now, we were back on track, with renewed vigour and determination.

So, apart from me learning to be less direct, what were the lessons learned and decisions made as a result of this outing?

Alec decided not to walk with a belly bag as it slumped too much and was uncomfortable. I decided to stick with mine; it had worked perfectly.

Our ascent pace was pretty consistent and reasonably quick for old boys, but if we could find the time and opportunity before the real thing we had to get more training in on rough descents.

As we had extended the distance we were covering in training, blisters were increasingly becoming a problem. I have a reasonably high pain threshold (I can even watch Emmerdale if Geoff forces me to) but blisters are sometimes almost more than I can bear. We resolved to keep a very close eye on our feet and make sure we were fully equipped with on the spot treatments for the event.

We knew what to expect in terms of car parking - or rather lack of it - at **Pen y Pass** *- and were able to put contingency plans in place.*

We recognised how important it was that things were stowed in appropriate pockets for each walk, so that it would not be necessary to stop to search for items in backpacks.

However, the main decision we made as a result of this trial was to change our route. We decided that we would climb **Snowdon** *using the* **Pyg Track** *and descend using the* **Miners' Track**.

These outings on the actual peaks we intended to climb were invaluable. Ideally, we would have climbed **Ben Nevis** too before the event but we just couldn't find the time. At least we'd walked the mountain in the past. And there was a need to keep things in perspective. As Bill Bryson pointed out, "If Ben Nevis were on the Appalachian Trail in New Hampshire, it would just squeak into the top ten. Snowdon would be swallowed without trace."

But not to have 'trialed' ourselves, our kit and at least some of our routes would have meant that we would not have realised our mistakes until the actual Challenge, which would have undoubtedly cost us comfort, effort and most importantly time. It may have made the difference between success and failure.

Our regular training regime continued as 'D Day' drew closer. However we still pushed ourselves as hard as time would permit. Alec undertook a twenty-five mile walk with his daughter Lynsey in the environs of **Dumfries** to test his stamina and came out of it well. I built up my regular training walks into eight, twelve and sixteen mile outings as often as time allowed during the last month. I kept up my training right up until 'D Day' minus 2. Alec stopped about a week before that, which he later thought was a bit too early.

Whatever, for better or for worse, preparation time had run out and we were soon about to do it for real …

So, how fit do you need to be?

Fairly fit is the answer. For sure, you don't have to be Olympic standard, but walking twenty four miles and climbing 9700 ft in twenty four hours is quite a challenge, even without the sleep deprivation. As well as decent general fitness, you need good muscle strength and stamina.

Also, getting experience of climbing hills in different weather conditions and tackling narrow mountain paths is important.

On the Three Peaks you will have to climb one of the mountains in the dark. So if you have never fellwalked at night, a night-time training outing can help a lot. Hardly anyone thinks of training in the dark.

Gym training and the occasional walk will just not cut the mustard. You will need to train on real mountains in real weather, the more the better, as well as undertaking a daily walking regime. Finding the time for training is the biggest difficulty for many.

If I had to pick a figure, I would say that six months is about the right period of time a normal, healthy, unfit person should reasonably allow to prepare from scratch. It can be done in less if you have mountain experience, or a decent starting level of fitness - Alec and I trained for four months.

In that period, I'd suggest you should walk regularly six or seven days a week, at a brisk four miles per hour. So, based upon our own regime, on the next page is a 26 week training plan. It would be a miracle if you went through the whole six months without missing a single scheduled session as a result of illness, injury or personal circumstances.

If you do have to interrupt the schedule, when you have recovered it's best to gradually pick it up at a point some days before you left off. All the figures represent walking miles, and assume a pace of four miles per hour. In order to ensure that distances are accurate I always prefer to tackle a measured 'out and back' route rather than a circular loop, but this is a personal choice.

An Example Training Schedule

	SUN	MON	TUE	WED	THUR	FRI	SAT
Week 1	4	4	4	4	4	4	4
Week 2	4	4	4	4	4	4	4
Week 3	4	4	4	4	4	4	4
Week 4	Hill walk	Rest day	4	4	4	4	8
Week 5	8	4	4	4	4	4	8
Week 6	8	4	4	4	4	4	8
Week 7	8	4	4	4	4	4	8
Week 8	Hill walk	Rest day	4	4	4	4	8
Week 9	12	4	4	4	4	4	8
Week 10	12	4	4	4	4	4	12
Week 11	12	4	4	4	4	4	12
Week 12	Hill walk	Rest day	4	4	4	4	12
Week 13	12	4	4	4	4	4	12
Week 14	12	4	4	4	4	4	12
Week 15	12	4	4	4	4	4	12
Week 16	12	4	4	4	4	4	12
Week 17	Long hill walk	Rest day	4	4	4	4	12
Week 18	12	4	4	4	4	4	12
Week 19	12	4	4	4	4	4	12
Week 20	12	4	4	4	4	4	12
Week 21	16	4	4	4	4	4	12
Week 22	Long hill walk	Rest day	4	4	4	4	12
Week 23	20	4	8	4	8	4	12
Week 24	16	4	8	4	8	4	12
Week 25	16	4	8	4	8	4	12
Week 26	4	4	4	4	Travel to start	Challenge	Challenge

"In preparation for battle, I have always found that plans are useless, but planning is indispensible."

Dwight D Eisenhower, General and US President.

Immediately the 'go' commitment had been made in February, my mind turned to the organisation needed for the challenge. The areas that needed to be planned were:

- the timing of the attempt,
- the walking routes,
- the road routes,
- the schedule,
- the roles and responsibilities of the support team,
- the equipment and supplies needed, and who would supply what,
- accommodation,
- the finances,
- the food and drink needed, and when and where it should be cooked and consumed,
- recording the event (photo and video),
- the ground rules for team operation.

Interestingly, because I voluntarily took charge of the planning and organisation, by default it seemed I became the team leader. The power of having a 'cunning plan' came into force.

This issue of leadership is important, I think. We didn't deal with it the best way. We allowed a leader to emerge, rather than agreeing it collectively. Fortunately, everyone was happy to accept it.

However it's done, it's important to have someone to at least coordinate all the pre-challenge activity and someone, maybe someone different, to lead on the hills.

Some of the basic logistical issues had to be resolved first.

Alec and I decided that in order to minimise the time spent walking during the hours of darkness,. we would have to undertake our attempt as close to the summer solstice as possible, when days are long, and if we were lucky the nights are almost non-existent in the North.

Another, but secondary consideration, was the phase of the moon. A full moon on a clear night would be a real boon. The dates we plumped for eventually were the 22nd and 23rd June, a Friday and Saturday. It would only be a quarter moon, but if we got our timings right we might hardly need to walk in the dark.

This choice meant that we would all have to gather on Thursday 21st, then travel to our starting point on the 22nd and complete the walk on the 23rd. We would stay over on that night at a local pub or hotel and head home on Sunday 24th.

*We quickly formed the opinion that it would be better to start with **Ben Nevis** and work our way south, than the opposite way. Not only does this sequence mean that you get the biggest climb out of the way first, while you're fresh both physically and mentally, but the timings allow you to minimise night walking.*

Our target times were 5½ hours on **Ben Nevis**, 3½ hours on **Scafell** and 3½ hours on **Snowdon**, a total of 12½ hours on the hills.

*Based upon information we gleaned from the internet (users.tinyonline.co.uk/richieev/tp was especially useful) and from web journey planners, we estimated our driving times to be 5½ hours from **Ben Nevis** to **Scafell Pike (Wasdale)**, and 4½ hours from **Wasdale** to **Pen y Pass**.*

Indeed, most mass organised Three Peak events now insist on applying a minimum drive time of ten hours even if in reality you do it quicker. This is to discourage speeding and risk taking of course, but as an unofficial team we had no such constraints. Nevertheless we used this rule of thumb for planning purposes. This meant that if we started at 4.00 p.m. in the afternoon, we would be down by 9.30 p.m.. Allowing for fifteen minutes 'messing around time' before and after every mountain, we would be off by 9.45 p.m.. A drive of 5½ hours would mean a 3.15 a.m. arrival at **Wasdale** and a 3.30 a.m. start.

Sunrise on the 23rd was forecast for 4.30 a.m., but from previous experience we knew that on a clear day at least, it starts to get light up to an hour beforehand. We would be back down and away to **Snowdon** by 7.15 a.m., arriving at **Pen y Pass** by 11.45 a.m. and on the hill by noon. Three-and-a-half hours up and down would see us complete the challenge by 3.30 p.m., after 23½ hours. Not a lot of slack, but worth a shot …

"Everywhere is walking distance if you have the time."

Steve Wright, American comedian and actor.

In order to fine tune our schedule we needed not just to decide on the sequence of the mountains, but the exact routes we would take up them.

BEN NEVIS

Ben Nevis Visitor Centre, Glen Nevis

*Although there are scrambling alternatives on Ben Nevis, the only practicable route for the challenge is the **Pony Track** which starts from the **Ben Nevis Visitor Centre** in **Glen Nevis**. There is ample parking and apparently all the big charity events are asked to start from here.*

*There is another start point a little further up the glen and on the opposite side of the **River Nevis** at **Achintee Farm** where the **Ben Nevis Inn** is also located. Parking is limited here, and it fills up quickly during the afternoons.*

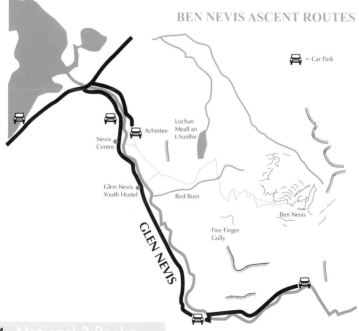

BEN NEVIS ASCENT ROUTES

= Car Park

Lochan
Meall an
t-Suidhe

Achintee

Nevis
Centre

Glen Nevis
Youth Hostel

Red Burn

Ben Nevis

Five Finger
Gully

GLEN NEVIS

*Finally, there is a third access point for the **Pony Track** otherwise called the **Tourist Track** and now officially the **Mountain Track** from the youth hostel in **Glen Nevis**. This is very steep until it meets the main path, and there is even less parking there, so we decided to go from **Achintee**.*

The Nevisside footpath

*In good weather the **Mountain Track** is clear on the ground for its whole length. It's even paved with huge boulders and slabs for much of its first half.*

However, in 1986 Alec and I had tackled the **West Highland Way**, and decided, as is traditional, to finish off our expedition by climbing the Ben. It was early June and the weather was warm in the valley with some high cloud. Dressed in T shirts, but properly equipped with spare gear, unlike many others on the path (high heels and carrier bags seemed to be the order of the day) - we climbed steadily past **Lochan Meall an t-Suidhe**, the '**Half-Way Lochan**' and noticed the air was getting chillier. By the time we reached the beginning of the zigzags the wind had risen and we were crossing substantial snowfields. The footpath disappeared under a blanket of snow over a foot thick, and soon the footprints of previous walkers faded away.

We were on our own now, all the day trippers had turned back or maybe wandered off an edge somewhere. We donned fleeces, waterproofs and balaclavas.

Higher still and we found ourselves in true white-out conditions, the first time I had ever been on a mountain and not been able to find the horizon. The ground and the sky were indistinguishable. A vicious wind had sprung up and was whipping up the snow into our faces and we were getting colder. We arrived on the summit plateau, which is well cairned, but the mist was so dense that we found that we lost sight of the last cairn before we could even spot the next one, which was a bit disconcerting. The only way we could proceed was by 'leap

A Ben Nevis cornice

frogging'.

The ground had levelled off now and we were wondering just how much further we had to go. Momentarily the mist lifted just for a split second - and revealed that Alec was standing on the brink of a precipitous gully that dropped away to our left. He was almost certainly standing on a cornice. Alec was no featherweight even then, so ever so gingerly he backtracked to firm ground. It was probably **Gardyloo Gully**, which is about 150 metres from the summit trig point, but to proceed in a straight line is certain death as one must dog-leg around the head of the gully. Somewhat shaken now, we decided that discretion was the better part of valour and headed for home. Even this was not easy though as the windblown snow had filled our footprints.

The end in sight

As we descended, the weather conditions reversed themselves and we progressively divested our clothing. Sitting outside the pub at the bottom, basking in the summer warmth with a pint in his hand Alec murmured, "I hope no one follows my footprints on the top..."

This made me laugh, but actually, we were both very sobered by the experience.

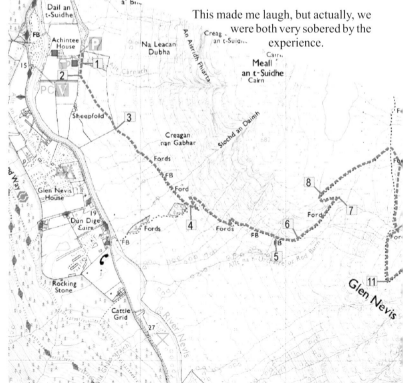

We'd been both quite foolish and very lucky. On a mountain like **Ben Nevis**, which has precipitous drops on several sides of its summit plateau, when ordinary fellwalkers find themselves in a whiteout, then retreat is indicated. These days GPS would make this safer and easier. You would just reverse your track log or - if you had not been recording it, your plotted route - and follow it down.

Most of us, however experienced, push our luck or do something crass on the hills from time to time. Assuming we escape death and injury, the crucial thing is to learn from it. I believe we did, and although we have never encountered identical circumstances since, I believe we would behave quite differently now. The legendary Edward Whymper, who on his 8th attempt successfully achieved the first ascent of the Matterhorn, said something salient after he lost four of his six climbing companions on the descent. "Climb if you will, but remember that courage and strength are nought without prudence and that a momentary negligence may destroy the happiness of a lifetime." And that from a man who continued to take on risky challenges.

Fortunately, despite the occasional stupidity of the hill-going public, most mountain rescue teams take a very non-judgmental attitude to people who find themselves in trouble. They recognise the frailty of the human decision-making process.

They understand that people love the hills and want to be in them, because they do too. And they know we make mistakes.

They are also incredibly patient - but firm - with people who really just want a guide down, rather than needing to be rescued. One mountain rescue team doesn't rush to deal with these situations so long as the weather isn't extreme and the party is well provisioned, reasoning that all they need is a bit more time to get down. Or alternatively, the party is offered the services of a professional guide who will turn out, meet them, and guide them down, all for about £200.

Alec had climbed the **Ben** many times since our scary experience, without incident. I had not. I still retained some residual nervousness that our challenge expedition could also encounter the conditions of June 1986.

As a footnote, it's worth noting that since 2010 much work has been undertaken to improve safety on the summit plateau. Dozens of confusing cairns have been removed. A few new strategically placed replacements now provide obvious and much more useful reference points. In particular the direction from the top of the zigzags to the summit is much more clearly cairned. In addition, more of the mountain track has been 'engineered'. This work is ongoing.

In the text that follows, Wp. denotes Waypoint. For full details and coordinates see Annex 2.

The Ben Nevis Inn and Achintee car park

*From the **Ben Nevis Visitor Centre (Glen Nevis)** car park follow the riverside path in the **Fort William** direction for a couple of hundred metres. This will bring you to a suspension footbridge over the **Nevis**. Turn right at the*

The view from the start of the Mountain Track at Achintee (Wp.1)

*other side and follow the path until it meets the main track at **Achintee**, just to the south of the **Ben Nevis Inn**.*

*From the **Achintee** car park*

The stile at Wp.3 to the open hillside

*and the **Ben Nevis Inn** the start of the path is obvious, through the gate at the end in front of the pub (Wp.1). After 50 metres (Wp.2) the path turns left up the hillside. You crest a rise and then cross a stile (Wp.3) at the corner of a fence, still heading in the same south-easterly direction.*

About two-thirds of a mile from the start, the youth hostel path joins from the right and the track undertakes a short zigzag (Wp.4), first left, then right. The path at this stage is well paved with huge rock slabs and it crosses two streams by metal footbridges (Wp.5)

The second of the metal bridges on the Ben Nevis Mountain Track

Shortly afterwards the path veers left (Wp.6) and then contours above the valley of the **Red Burn**. Soon the path zigzags (Wp.7) left, then right, as it climbs up the valley side, trending right (Wp.8) and easing as it nears the **Halfway Lochan** plateau. It then makes a beeline for the head of the corrie

Halfway Lochan - which is not quite halfway!

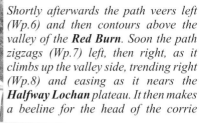

where it crosses the **Red Burn** (Wp.9).

There it turns sharp right, soon fording the **Red Burn** (Wp.10), after which it becomes rougher and steeper.

The famous zigzags start now with a left turn (Wp.11), then right (Wp.12), then left (Wp.13), then right (Wp.14), then left (Wp.15), then right (Wp.16), then left (Wp.17), then right (Wp.18), until the slope eases. At this point (Wp.19) the correct route takes a 90° turn to the left, but there is another branch which goes straight on. DO NOT TAKE THIS PATH AS IT LEADS TO **COIRE GHAINHNAIM** AND THE HEAD OF **FIVE FINGER GULLY**.

The main route eases now and becomes cairned, signaling the final pull up to the summit plateau. There is almost always a patch of snow here, right up until July. Follow the well-defined path which is bordered now by slightly larger rocks, until the summit plateau is reached, indicated by a leveling of the incline. It's worth paying particular attention to the angle of approach, so that the way down can be found afterwards when it's easy to become disorientated in mist.

The path skirts precipitous gullies (Wp.20) at the left hand edge of the plateau until **Gardyloo Gully** is passed. Then, at a cluster of three large well-built cairns, the path turns sharp left (Wp.21) for the last 150 metres to the summit (Wp.22).

In mist, to descend safely it's necessary to reverse the dog leg approach in order to clear the head of **Gardyloo Gully**. Take 150 long paces (metres) on bearing, 231° towards the three cairns then turn to 282° and follow that until the zigzags are regained. Once again, this is more accurate if

SCAFELL PIKE

Scafell Pike presents three realistic alternative ascent routes. The first and most popular starts at **Wasdale**, from the entrance lane to the **National Trust Campsite** (Wp.1). Parking may be possible in the lay-by at the roadside.

Cross the road and follow the track over the bridge past the campsite car park, over a second bridge (Wp.2), to **Brackenclose**. Take the path up the side of **Lingmell Gill** to a narrow footbridge (Wp.3), turn left over it and cross the gill.

Start of Scafell Pike path at Brackenclose

*Once across turn right (Wp.4) and climb a few metres to a gate (Wp.5). Once through the gate, climb more steeply now with **Lingmell Gill** to your right, until you arrive at a second gate (Wp.6).*

Alongside Lingmell Gill - the early stages

Crossing Lingmell Gill

Made path up Brown Tongue

*Continue in this same general direction, watching out for a 90° right turn in the path (Wp.7) where it crosses back over the gill. Once across, turn half left up **Brown Tongue**.*

When the path reaches a large cairn (Wp.8), trend left again up a made path of boulders. The path then diverges

Fork in path (Wp.10)

*(Wp.9). Take the left hand fork which leads to the beginning of **Hollow Stones**.*

*After a while the path becomes gravelly and it starts a series of zigzags (Wp.10). After these zigzags it eases and then veers right as it nears **Lingmell Col**. Another couple of hundred metres further on (Wp.11) the path takes a 90° turn to the right and starts to climb steeply again.*

.. a huge rectangular boulder ..

This is the final pull up to the summit. As soon as you start this climb, on your immediate right you should see - in daylight anyway - a huge rectangular boulder with a small cairn on top.

The path now climbs through some rocky outcrops, twisting first right (Wp.12) and then left. Even in a head-torch beam though, the path has a different hue from the surrounding rocks. The gradient then eases and the way crosses a boulder field (Wp.13) before heading across a cairned slope of loose rock and finally attaining the summit (Wp.14).

*The significant drawback in using this route is the long drive - up to an extra hour - around the western edge of the Lake District, **Wasdale** being one of the most remote valleys.*

*Once there though, this path is the shortest way up the mountain, albeit the steepest, gaining 885m (2900ft) in just under three miles. The other two routes start from **Seathwaite Farm** at the end of **Borrowdale**. From the car park in the lane, the path goes straight past the farmhouse and follows the main track easily up to and over **Stockley Bridge**.*

*Then the first alternative turns to the right and continues more steeply up **Styhead Gill**. After passing **Styhead Tarn** and the mountain rescue kit at **Sty Head**, the route turns left, then, at a dip, right onto the **Corridor Route**, through the crags, over **Skew Gill** - where there is a little rocky scramble out of the defile - on to **Greta Gill**, shortly after which watch out for a fork in the path. Take the right hand fork (straight ahead) which will take you on to **Lingmell Col**. At the col, the way turns left for the final climb to the summit which you will reach after a total of just under five miles.*

SCAFELL PIKE ASCENT ROUTES

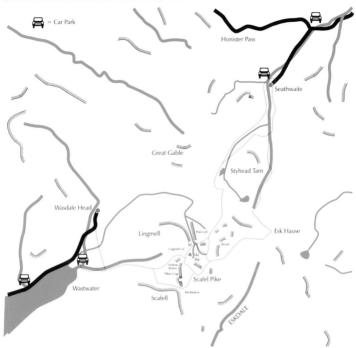

= Car Park

Honister Pass

Seathwaite

Great Gable

Styhead Tarn

Wasdale Head

Lingmell

Pass Gill

Esk Hause

Lingmell col

Broad

Hollow Stones

Pikes Crag

Scafel Pike

Wastwater

Mickledore

Scafell

ESKDALE

*The second possible route is a little more direct and a little shorter at four and a quarter miles long. From **Stockley Bridge**, carry straight on up **Grains Gill**, trending right up to **Ruddy Gill** where you turn left and then meet the main **Sty Head** to **Langdale** path.*

*Turn left and follow it towards **Esk Hause**, where a short cut turns right and a clear and easy path takes you up behind **Great End**. There is a steepish rocky haul up onto the **Ill Crag** plateau, then a bouldery walk over to **Broad Crag** which you pass to your right, a drop down to **Broad Crag Col** and then a final pull up to **Scafell Pike** summit.*

*Either of these routes is likely to take between forty-five and seventy-five minutes more to complete than the **Wasdale Path**. In addition the **Corridor Route** is rough underfoot and its beginning from **Sty Head** can be difficult to find in the dark or mist.*

*Finding one's way off **Scafell Pike** summit - unless you use a GPS - can be surprisingly tricky. It's easy to forget the direction of approach (cairns abound) and paths don't become clear for a few hundred yards in any direction, so as a failsafe, these are the bearings you should take from the summit shelter:-*

- *For **Lingmell Col**: 231 degrees, then the path trends down to the right.*
- *For **Esk Hause**: 50 degrees, then just below some shelter walls turn left on a level path and then more steeply downhill to the **Broad Crag Col**.*

*There is a final alternative strategy which some people adopt, and that is to walk up from **Wasdale** and descend to **Borrowdale**, with the drivers driving round to **Seathwaite** while the walkers are on the hills. We decided upon the **Wasdale** route up and down, preferring to spend the extra time sleeping in the car rather than sweating on the hillside.*

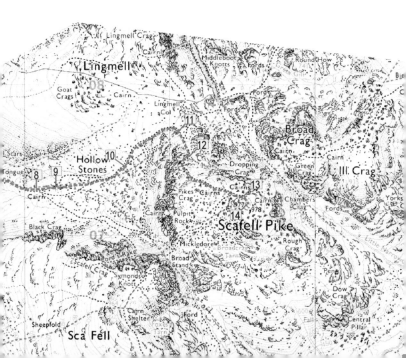

There is another important factor to take into consideration at **Wasdale** in particular, the environmental impact. This is perhaps best described by Guy Newbold, a walker and climber who lives and works in **Wasdale**. He wrote the following article in 2002 expressing a local's view of the damage inflicted in the name of good causes.

*"A lot has been said recently about the impact of the Three Peak 'challenges' held on **Scafell Pike**, **Ben Nevis** and **Snowdon**. The main problem with the debate is that most can only base their observations on individual events and there are few who are able to comment on it as a year-long phenomenon without being accused of vested interest and a local anti-tourist type of attitude.*

*Well, I am a local of **Wasdale**, but I also make my living from visitors to the fells, so my viewpoint is as balanced as you could hope for. I wasn't born here, instead taking the route of the 'off comer' settling in the area because of a deep love for the Cumbrian fells. I'm a climber, a walker, and a runner and a kayaker and perhaps my view may be of interest to some? Thousands of people have done the Three Peaks challenge; some have done it as part of a large organised group and some as part of a smaller team. The rules are pretty random, some set a time constraint on completing the event - usually either 24 hours or three days - and some require you to start at certain points away from the peaks themselves. Whatever the rules most people arriving to climb **Scafell Pike** have already climbed one of the other peaks and most choose to begin from **Wasdale** as it represents the shortest possible route up and down.*

*But before we get into the debate. let's get a few facts straight. The majority of people will try to climb all three of the peaks in 24 hours. As a result of the above most will arrive at **Scafell Pike** during the night. The summer months around the longest day are the most popular times of the year although from May to October you will find groups doing it every weekend. Most people do the event as part of a large sponsored event raising money for a charity. A large percentage will not be regular fell goers, as they are doing it solely to raise funds for a good cause. We are not talking about a couple of hundred people spread out over the year, it is hundreds of people each night ... 200 people using a path in one hour do ten times the amount of damage as 200 people do using the same path over the course of a week. Large numbers of people arriving in the middle of the night by minibus cannot do so quietly. **Wasdale** has no public toilets, but people still need to go even if there isn't one available.*

Some charities pay event companies to organise the events for them, the more the better for the company and the charity. It isn't just a fundraiser, it's big business. 2,000 eventers at £100 a head - someone's getting rich and it's not the charity.

So those are the facts, what's to debate? Well the problem is the event keeps on getting more and more popular as it raises more and more money for good causes. This has meant that patience is now low among locals who can spend almost all their weekends awake, visitors are not returning to the B and Bs, hotels and campsites are empty as they too don't want to be kept awake and finally, the environment is starting to suffer.

Wasdale is a remarkable place, remote and beautiful. It doesn't have the facilities of *Ben Nevis* or *Snowdon* and that's half its charm; it is still a remote wilderness. *Scafell Pike* doesn't have one main path and so there isn't a continuous pitched and paved route to the summit. The increased traffic is concentrated in time periods and so causes much more damage than the same number of feet spread over a week. The result is that paths are now becoming deep ruts 30 to 40 feet wide. Even the old *Brown Tongue Path* which was redirected is now suffering and is slowly returning the large muddy scar it was before the renovation work was done 10 years ago as the sheer number of walkers means many ignore the new, pitched path.

And the valley floor is fairing no better either, there are no adequate toilet facilities as there is no mains sewage, the result is little piles topped with tissue behind every wall and tree. The water too is in great demand as it all comes from private wells, which are all too easily drained by a team of thirsty Three Peakers. Litter now piles up during the night and the verges and green spaces are becoming bogs as the hundreds of minibuses churn them all up, even spaces reserved only for emergency vehicles are used as base camps during the night.

Wasdale is taking a beating, and is not always a pretty or pleasant place to be. So what can be done? well relatively little actually. More parking can not be provided, nor can toilets and bins, as someone has to pay to install, equip, clean and empty them. That's without considering the effect they would have on the whole feel of *Wasdale* and the detrimental effect on the breathtaking natural scenery.

The fells paths can't all be pitched, as it would be hugely expensive and impact on the wild beauty of the hills. And try as they might hundreds of people booting up and preparing for a walk can't do so in silence. Rubbish will always be created try as they might to stop it but tell someone that they are doing something for charity and the ends will always justify the means.

So who can do something; the National Park? National Trust? Government? Well in a word, no. You can't deny people the freedom of the fells, access is for all at all times of the day or night and long may it continue.

To my mind the event needs to be controlled not on site, but in the planning stages and before. Charities need to aware of the damage they are causing and made to pay for the repairs, or installation of facilities. The event needs to be controlled so that it isn't going on during the night and large groups don't pick the same weekend. But mainly and most positively the charities need to take a responsible stance and find something else to do instead. Sit in a bath of baked beans, don't talk for a month, shave your head, anything, but don't put 2,000 people on *Scafell* on a Saturday night! People who might volunteer to do it and charities that want the money *need to think.*

*Please come to **Wasdale** and perhaps do the Three Peaks - you and a few friends - just don't come with one or two hundred close personal pals and definitely not in the middle of the night. "*

We concurred with some points that Gary Newbold had made, in particular about the rubbish and the toilet habits of some challengers. In 2010 some portacabin toilets and large dumpster type refuse bins were place close to the **Wasdale Head Inn** for the use of three peakers. On our last visit to **Wasdale** they were filthy and overflowing, quite obviously overwhelmed and abused by their users. But we took issue with others. The only way for us to avoid all of the above problems was not to do the Three Peaks at all, which we were determined to do. We reasoned that we were relatively low impact, we were a small group, we would make a real effort to be quiet. We would time our toilet stops to avoid adding to the effluent problems of the valley - hoping that our digestive systems would cooperate.

SNOWDON

*Snowdon also has three possible walking routes, although ninety five per cent of Three Peakers must surely opt for either the **Pyg Track** or the **Miners' Track**, both of which start from 360m (1100ft) above sea-level at the **Pen y Pass** car park. All the paths are clear on the ground with no route-finding difficulties.*

SNOWDON ASCENT ROUTES

*The **Pyg Track** starts from the right hand side of the car park behind the Information Centre (Wp.1). It rises steeply initially, just to the right of some rocky outcrops (Wp.2). It eases for a while, then steepens again before veering right (Wp.3). The path then turns left (Wp.4) and heads up to **Bwlch y Moch** (Wp.5) where it crosses to the other side of the ridge and then over a double stile. At this pass the path forks; the one to the left is the **Pyg Track** which now inclines steadily across the southern flanks of **Crib Goch**. The right-hand fork heads for its summit.*

*After two more miles heading in the same generally westerly direction, it reaches the junction with the **Miners' Track** (Wp.6) which comes in from the left. The way then rises steeply up a series of zigzags (Wp.7) to the col at the **Pigtop Pillar** (Wp.8). The route turns left here and the summit (Wp.9) is then no more than an easy fifteen minute walk.*

The **Miners' Track** leaves the left-hand corner of the same car park through a gate helpfully labelled **'Miners' Track'** (Wp.1). The path is gravelled and rises gradually for three miles, wending its way through the floor of the cwm.

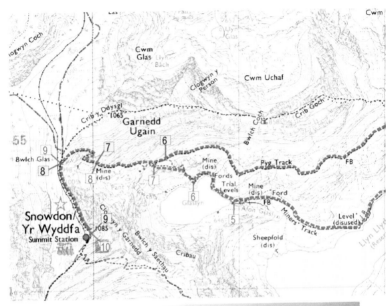

At the first bend it turns right (Wp.2) passing **Llyn Teyrn** and then as it nears the causeway across **Llyn Lydaw** it turns right to cross it (Wp.3). (The path that goes straight on heads up to **Y Lliwedd**). At the end of the causeway (Wp.4) turn left, heading again in a south-westerly direction. The next landmark is **Glaslyn** (Wp.5).

At the end of the valley (Wp.6) it all changes and the path rises abruptly like a staircase until it meets the **Pyg Track** (Wp.7)

Pyg Track - disappearing into the mist

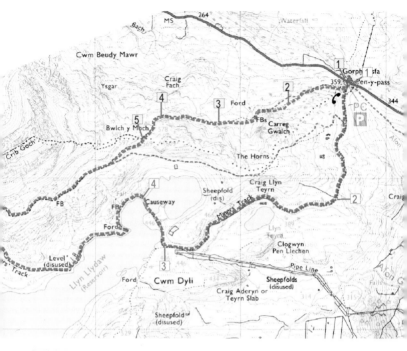

Last few steps to the Pigtop Pillar

*which comes in from the right. The rest of the route is the same as the **Pyg Track**; up the zigzags (Wp.8) to the **Pigtop Pillar** (Wp.9), then left to the summit (Wp.10).*

*The **Llanberis Path** is the only other feasible one. It is the easiest and most gently graded of all the routes, but is also the longest at five miles. It starts at the first side road above the **Snowdon Mountain Railway Station** in **Llanberis**.*

This lane leads at its end to the path proper, which turns left up the mountain, and continues as a blazed trail all the way to the top. The rough and stony path runs alongside the railway on one side or another all the way to the top and in my view is absolute purgatory. With plenty of time in hand, some Three Peakers might want to use it in descent. Why anyone

Miners' Track crossing Llyn Lydaw causeway

would choose to ascend this way mystifies me.

*We decided to take the **Pyg Track** up and the **Miners' Track** down. With the benefit of experience, next time - and there will be a next time - we would probably follow the **Miners' Track** both up and down.*

As a footnote to this section, with its emphasis on navigation and path-finding, I understand from a friend of mine that some charities provide marshals at frequent intervals on their selected (compulsory) routes in order to keep their fundraising fellwalkers on track. During the hours of darkness the marshals are even equipped with 'glow flares'.

One can see that it's in the interests of the charity to ensure that none of their human cash-generators get lost, but it must take something away from the challenge and the essence of the event.

Six THE ROAD ROUTES

*"Have you ever noticed that anyone driving slower than you is an idiot
and anyone driving faster than you is a maniac?"*

George Carlin, comedian, actor and author.

Driving times may not 'make' the challenge, but they can certainly break it.

All the nervousness and excitement of the uncertainty associated with road and traffic conditions adds to the tension of the challenge. So route selection is important. These were our choices. And we were lucky; they worked like a dream.

*From **Ben Nevis** one heads back towards **Fort William** but avoid the town centre by taking the bypass - straight over at the mini roundabout - and then head south on the **A82**, passing **Corran Ferry**, and crossing the **Ballachullish Bridge**. Immediately after the bridge turn left - still on the **A82** - bypassing **Glencoe** village to the left and following the main road up the pass and across **Rannoch Moor**. Then on through **Bridge of Orchy** and **Tyndrum** to **Crianlarich**.*

*Here there is a choice to be made. Either turn right, continuing on the **A82** down the side of **Loch Lomond** - which is shorter, but narrow and twisty so as a result it can be very slow - then just after **Dumbarton** taking the **A898** over the **Erskine Bridge**, picking up the **M8** through **Glasgow**, then joining the new stretch of the **M74** at **junction 22**.*

*Or, alternatively carry straight ahead onto the **A85** which will take you to **Lochearnhead**, where you pick up the **A84** to **Calendar** and **Doune** and on to the **M9** at **junction 10**, just north of **Stirling**. Heading south, at the next junction you take the **M80** which becomes the **A80** dual carriageway. Follow this to the **M73** and follow that until it joins the **M74**. On either route, you should keep following signs for **Carlisle** and 'The South'.*

*We chose the **A82** to **Glasgow**. As it was late evening, there was little traffic, we had no delays and made excellent time. Either way, once on the **M74** you'll probably need a fuel and toilet stop. We used **Bothwell** services, but there are good services further on at **Gretna** if you want to get more miles under your belt. This is actually a better point to fuel up because if time gets short on the way to **Snowdon**, you'll have enough fuel to keep going. Then it's back onto the **M74** all the way to the **M6**. At **junction 44** of the **M6** take the **A7** into **Carlisle**. At around midnight the roads are quiet.*

*From **Carlisle** town centre, follow signs for the **A595**, heading towards **Workington** and then **Whitehaven**. At **Thursby** roundabout take the second left to continue on the **A595** through **Mealsgate** and **Bothel**, to* *meet the **A66** outside of **Cockermouth**. Turn right onto the **A66** for a short distance, before following signs again for the **A595** toward **Whitehaven**. As you approach **Whitehaven**, keep left to avoid the town centre, staying on the **A595**. Carry on through **Egremont**, **Calderbridge** and **Ponsonby**. Shortly afterwards take a left turning signposted to **Gosforth**. Head into the village, then at the main junction turn left towards **Wasdale**. Bear next left and continue to a junction where you should bear right, up a very steep road. Carry on through Nether **Wasdale** and turn left at the next junction, signposted for **Wasdale Head**.*

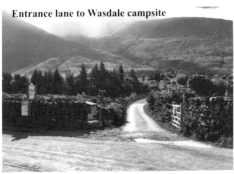

Entrance lane to Wasdale campsite

*Wast Water will soon appear on your right. Continue over several humpback bridges and about a mile before **Wasdale Head** turn right at the **National Trust Campsite**. Follow this track through the car park until it ends at the beginning of a footpath. Park here.*

It's worth noting that in 2008 a £5 charge for parking has been introduced for non-campers. In any case, parking here may not be possible as the car park is often closed on summer nights from 8.30 p.m. until 7.30 a.m. to prevent disturbance to the camp site, In which case, park at the roadside lay-by and as soon as the gate opens, move to the above position.

*So then it's up and down **Scafell Pike**, back into the car and off you go again. Head back from **Wasdale** to **Nether Wasdale** and turn left at the junction, signposted for **Santon Bridge**. At **Santon Bridge** follow signs for **Eskdale Green**. At the end of **Eskdale Green** village, turn right for **Ulpha**, following a twisty minor road to meet the main **A595** near **Duddon Bridge**. Turn left onto the **A595**.*

*At **Grizebeck**, bear left onto the **A5092**. Follow this to **Greenodd** where you turn left onto the **A590**, which will take you all the way to the **M6**.*

*Join the **M6** at **junction 36** and head south all the way to **junction 20**. This is the **M6/M56** intersection. Follow the **M56** signposted 'North Wales and Chester' and carry on all the way to the end of the **M56** which ends at a large roundabout and turn left onto the **A5117**. Then it's straight over at the next roundabout, still on the **A5117**. At traffic lights, bear left staying on the dual carriageway, which now becomes the **A550 Queensferry**. Stay on this dual carriageway which becomes the **A494** and then the **A55**, following signs for **Conwy** or **Bangor** The coast road has varying speed limits, but the only permanent speed cameras (as of July 2008) are concentrated around **Conwy** and **Colwyn Bay**. This is a fast piece of road where you can make good time.*

*The **A55** bypasses **Conwy**, after which you should follow signs for 'Bangor', until you reach the **A5** turn off. Take this sliproad and turn left at the roundabout towards **Bethesda**, then immediately right onto the **A4244**. Just after this turn there is a petrol station on the right. (We stopped here for a toilet break. It has good facilities). At the next roundabout, turn left, still on the **A4244**, following signs for **Llanberis**. At the T junction with the **A4086**, turn left. Carry on along the main road which bypasses **Llanberis** centre on the right.*

*Follow the road to the summit of **Pen y Pass** four miles further on and turn right into the turning area of the car park. If possible which is unlikely - park here. If not, drop off your walkers, and return to **Llanberis**. Return to **Pen y Pass** three and a half hours later to pick them up, hopefully triumphant. After this, road routes don't matter - you've either done it - or not.*

It's worth checking 'roadworks and accidents' websites, both in advance and just as you depart. We used the following ones:

www.trafficscotland.org

www.highways.gov.uk/trafficinfo

www.rac.co.uk/web/trafficnews

So after all this agonising over routes, our schedule looked like this:

Thursday 21 June

- Steve and family drive to **Darlington** (Geoff's place). Depart home at 09.00 arrive **Darlington** 13.00

- Mark to meet with Geoff and Steve at 13.00

- Depart **Darlington** by 15.00 arriving at **Dumfries** (Alec's place) by 17.30

Friday 22 June

- Depart **Dumfries** by 09.00

- Arrive at **Fort William** (**Achintee** car park) by 15.00 on Friday having had lunch on the way at the **Clachaig Inn, Glen Coe**.

- Steve and Alec start walking up **Ben Nevis** at 16.00.

- Total time: 5 hours 30. Summit by 3 hours. Target time back at base 21.30. Drivers to be ready to leave by 20.45 - just in case of a miracle time by walkers!

- Depart **Glen Nevis** by 22.00 latest.

Saturday 23 June

- Arrive **Wasdale** 03.30 latest

- Steve and Alec start walking up **Scafell Pike** by 03.30 latest. (2900 ft of ascent)

- Total time: 3 hours 30. Summit by 2 hours. Latest target time back at base 07.00 but drivers to be ready to leave by 06.30

- Depart **Wasdale** by 07.30 latest. Arrive **Snowdon** 12.00 latest.

- Steve and Alec start walking up **Snowdon** from **Pen y Pass** car park by 12.00 latest.

- Total time: 3 hours 30. Summit by 2 hours. Target time back at base 15.30.

Seven CREATING 'THE PLAN'

"A goal without a plan is just a wish."

Antoine de Saint-Exupery, writer

With the schedule now sorted, our minds turned to the support activities that were necessary to make our challenge bid not only successful, but enjoyable. Very quickly we realised that what we wanted was not drivers, but in the truest sense of the word 'supporters'. Alec and I started to think about roles and responsibilities and came up with this list, not entirely tongue in cheek.

Roles: driver, navigator, cook, valet, nurse.

Responsibilities:
- To get us to the start points - in safety - on or before schedule.
- To provide food and drinks - hot and cold - at specific points and times
- To organise and reorganise the vehicle so that equipment is always accessible when needed.
- To help us kit up before each mountain.
- To encourage us and absorb moans, groans and bitching from walkers
- To maintain good humour and act as a foil for the walkers' sad witticisms
- To congratulate us heartily when we succeeded.

Alec also decided that Geoff should be responsible for providing preventative first-aid before each mountain and therefore should apply Vaseline to Alec's sensitive parts to prevent chafing … I decided that Alec should inform Geoff himself.

After enjoying this brainstorming process perhaps more than we should have done, we came up with another idea. How about making a 'video diary' of the event? I could provide a camcorder and tripod, and then we'd have a permanent record for posterity. Eat your heart out Ellen MacArthur! The idea was ratified.

Our intention had been to have a day out in the hills with Mark and Geoff some time before the challenge so that we could get to know Mark in a relaxed situation. But because of other commitments we just couldn't make it happen. However, on one occasion when I was in **Darlington** on other business, Geoff and Sue arranged for me to meet Mark briefly at their place. He seemed friendly enough, a decent bloke in his mid thirties.

Of course we did have to secure the agreement of both of our volunteers to their rather extended job description. This turned out to be no problem at all, mainly because both Mark and Geoff are flexible and easy-going. But early on I had also started to document a 'Challenge Plan' that evolved

through four versions before the actual event. Mark and Geoff calmly accepted - by and large - their expanding responsibilities described therein.

We also needed - and received - lots of 'back-office' support from sisters Chris (my wife) and Sue (Geoff's wife). Because we needed multiple flasks for hot food and drinks, Sue had commissioned her retired mother-in-law Sybil to scour every car boot sale for miles. We ended up with four extra flasks all for about 50p!

The plan eventually specified just about everything that needed to be done, by whom and with what. In addition to detailing accommodation, routes, timings and responsibilities, it listed every item of equipment, food and drink needed, and who would provide each of them. It specified the content and times of meal breaks. Just as importantly it spelled out the ground-rules that we would all operate to. These ground-rules evolved over the months preceding the Challenge. The final version was as follows:

Ground-rules

- All monies payable will be made to Steve by 2 June 07. An allowance of £20 per head for the final dinner will be included for each participant. (Any under/overspend will be adjusted on Sunday morning). Steve will settle the hotel bill, and will forward the fuel allowance to Geoff by cheque in ample time before the event.

- Walkers will walk together (ish!) on the mountains. In particular, both walkers will leave the summit area of **Ben Nevis** together.

Should one walker become injured on a mountain and the other wishes to continue, then both walkers will return to the car together. Thereafter, the expedition will proceed as planned, with the remaining walker attempting the challenge. Should one walker become injured on the final mountain (**Snowdon**), if the injured walker is safe and is able to get off the mountain alone, the remaining walker will continue with the challenge. If either or both walkers fail in the challenge, a new date will be set to repeat the challenge later this year.

- Alec has chosen not to walk with a belly bag, Steve will do so. Whatever the case, walkers must be properly organised, so that proper clothing is worn at the beginning of each mountain and items are stowed in appropriate pockets for each walk, so that it is not necessary to stop to search for items in backpacks on the walk.

- Walkers will undertake at least 3 minutes of warm up/down stretches at the beginning and end of each ascent .

- At the first suspicion of the development of a blister, walkers will stop to apply the appropriate treatment.

- Walkers will not stop for meal or drink breaks on the mountains, but will eat and drink on the move. Drinks will be taken from platypuses.

- No more than 5 minutes will be spent on the summit of each mountain, during which time photos will be taken.

- Geoff will pass on progress texts to Chris and Ve (Steve and Alec's wives) as each mountain is descended (Down 1, Down 2, Down 3).

- Drivers are responsible for basic vehicle checks: oil, water, washer bottle etc. Geoff to fuel up before the start.

- One overnight bag per person is permitted, with the minimum items allowed (toiletries and underwear) as space will be very tight.

- Drivers commit to being at the agreed spot and ready to drive the moment the walkers arrive back at the rendezvous, with all provisions prepared and equipment packed away. When possible, walkers descending mountains will phone the drivers 40 minutes before ETA. (This will not be possible at **Wasdale** where there is no mobile phone signal).

- Drivers will agree between themselves when to changeover during journeys. These should be at times which will cause minimum delay to the expedition. Drivers should have a plentiful supply of ready change for any bridge or tunnel tolls.

- A video diary of the event will be made. Drivers will be responsible for recording the walkers' departures and arrivals, without the need for repeat takes. Any proceeds from 'You've Been Framed' will be split between all parties. Steve will copy the film onto a video cassette for each participant after the event.

- Fun will be had by all, and the piss will be taken at every opportunity.

Email proved a boon in keeping our geographically dispersed team up to date with the latest plans. However, as time grew close for the off, I needed to know that everyone had prepared everything that they needed to.

We therefore agreed that we would all have a telephone conference call three weeks before the event, to take stock. We categorised equipment under two headings: 'stashed' (equipment sourced and put to one side) and 'sorted' (packed and ready to go). This certainly proved its value; Alec, Sue, Mark, Chris and myself were pretty much all organised; Geoff was his usual laid back self,

"Yes, yes, don't worry Stevie," (only Geoff is allowed to call me Stevie), "It'll be alright".

Nevertheless, it did galvanise him into getting his responsibilities finalised over the coming days. Either that, or my sister-in-law Sue had galvanised him. Our expedition seemed to have caught her imagination and she took an evident pride in making sure everything was spot on. By 'D Day' minus 2 everyone had delivered what they needed to.

Last minute activities included the purchasing and preparation of perishable foodstuffs. Chris had cooked and then deep frozen a beef stew for our supper on Friday night, and a special breakfast mix, also frozen, of Old Spot sausages, bacon and baked beans. These were to be transported in an electric cool box in the car and re-heated by our support team at the appropriate times.

It seemed we were ready to go.

The full challenge plan including equipment list can be seen at Annex 1.

*"There are three kinds of men: the one that learns by reading;
the few who learn by observation;
the rest of them have to pee on the electric fence for themselves."*

Will Rogers, actor, cowboy, humourist

In fine weather Chris, Nicole and I drove north to **Darlington** to rendezvous with Geoff and Mark at Geoff's place. Even Nicole was excited by what was going on:-

"Will Uncle Geoff be ready to go when we arrive Daddy?"
"I expect so darling," Fingers crossed …

The video recording started the moment we drove into Geoff's street, capturing our arrival and then subsequent moments of pre-expedition relaxation while Geoff, Mark and I tried to decide upon nicknames for each of us. I became 'Shackleton', Geoff became 'Oates' (he was always going outside for some time - usually for a smoke), Mark became 'Hillary', but Alec we struggled over. Eventually he was named 'Hamish' after the wiry and aged Scottish mountaineer Hamish MacInnes. We thought this was particularly appropriate as MacInnes was in the first party to ascend **Ben Nevis** by the **Zero Gully** in 1957.

Geoff and I did a last check of weather forecasts. *The Mountain Weather Information Service at* www.mwis.org.uk *is particularly good.* The weather forecast was not favourable; cloudy with sunny spells and frequent heavy showers. The cloud base could get as low as 300m/1000ft. Still, for better or worse we were committed now.

The car was fully loaded by 2.15 p.m. and we were ready to depart for **Dumfries** by 2.45 p.m. At this point Geoff produced a piece of kit that was to prove a source of laughter, a thorn in our side, and could even have destroyed our mission; a borrowed sat-nav.

Geoff, despite months of preparation time had not been able to trial the kit so this was the first run live. The journey went fine with the sat-nav's bossy voice being irritating but at least accurate. Until the outskirts of **Dumfries** that was, when it started to give errant directions. Despite my knowing the way like the back of my hand, Geoff chose to obey the siren in the box. As a result we took diversions via a Lidl car park and Halfords - not the direct route to say the least.

This was my first experience of the phenomenon of technology being so sacrosanct that its adherent dismisses the evidence of proven knowledge and even their own eyes. Actually, it was a good laugh at this stage of the adventure, but I was already getting nervous that if Geoff continued in the same vein during the challenge, we could come badly unstuck. I'd prepared laminated road route-cards for the drivers with guidance notes included and I was keen to ensure that we stuck to the exact detail of the researched and agreed route.

The first task on arrival at Alec's was to re-pack the car, incorporating his gear with the rest. Geoff had removed the parcel shelf and just as well as we were stacked up to the roof, without an inch to spare. At least we managed to keep the rear seats clear though, which would be essential if Alec and I were to have a chance of getting any sleep.

Then it was a beer or two, dinner and out to the pub. However, before we went out I cajoled my fellow adventurers into a final briefing, which they tolerated with varying levels of attention. At the pub, a Scotland versus England pool tournament eased us into a really enjoyable, and it has to be said alcoholic evening, getting to bed at about 12.30 a.m.. Incidentally, Scotland (Alec & I) won 9 - 2.

"Keep your feet on the ground, your eyes on the hills and never ever give up hope."
John Garnett, Director, The Industrial Society, 1962-86.

When I awoke at 6.00 a.m. the next morning with a nagging throb in my forehead, I realised that this was not the best start to D-Day and it was little consolation to realise that all the others felt similarly fragile. On top of that it was lashing down outside. But we had things to do. As Ve cooked us a slap-up Scottish breakfast complete with tattie scones, we all made up the food and sandwiches for the challenge. There were mountains of buttered rolls and filled rolls with four different fillings, plus pies, pasties, flapjacks. I started to suspect that we had over-catered. We certainly wouldn't go hungry.

Breakfast was greedily consumed and we started to feel better. Before nine o'clock we were on our way.

Within half an hour we had left the rain behind and started to enjoy the journey. Driving through **Glasgow**, that damned sat-nav tried to take us on a wild goose chase, but insistent cries of protest from Alec and I persuaded Geoff to ignore it.

It was a thoroughly pleasant day now and for Mark especially, who'd never been north of the border before, the scenery along **Loch Lomondside** and on to **Glen Coe** was stunning. We stopped at a roadside coffee shop. As we were leaving I paid the bill and the proprietor - as she must do a hundred times a day - asked where we were heading next. I explained our mission and she told me about her own N3P attempt the previous year. Then she said,

"We get a lot of Three Peakers through here."

Clachaig Inn, Glen Coe

Storm clouds gather at Glen Nevis

"So, can you tell whether they're going to make it?"
"Yeah, pretty much," she said.
"So what about us?" I asked, gesturing at myself and Alec. She looked at us in turn.
"Yeah, you'll do it alright," she replied …. but she didn't hold my eyes ….
"Good luck guys." she said as we left.

For Alec and I, this area was our old stomping ground and our return stimulated a raft of reminiscences. We stopped for lunch at the famous **Clachaig Inn** at **Glen Coe**. It had been many years since I had been there and I remembered the bar as an atmospheric climbers' haunt. Unfortunately it was empty, and had deteriorated a good deal since then. Alec and I felt slightly embarrassed to have taken Geoff and Mark there. Grubby, dank and painted in dark gloomy hues, the style could perhaps have been described as 'fin de siécle Punk'.

We made it to **Fort William** by 2.30 p.m., drove along the High Street thronged with Japanese tourists and found our way to **Achintee**. There were only a few cars dotted around the car park, but within minutes it started to fill up with minibuses, vans and cars as more and more 'challengers' and their support teams arrived. One driver turned in with an empty minibus - the walkers were arriving later by train.

"Which one's **Ben Nevis**?" he asked.
"The highest one," replied Alec.

There were shades of the **Snowdon** conversation here, but this time Alec couldn't retain his deadpan face and we all burst into laughter, including the driver fortunately. In fact, you can't see 'the Ben' from **Achintee**; it's hidden away to the left around of **Meall an t'-Suidhe**. The driver got back in his bus, reversed out of his space and promptly collided with another minibus.

Ben Nevis from the campsite

"I'm glad he's not driving us," murmured Alec. "That van'll be written off by Wales."

The weather now was warm and humid, with huge dark threatening storm clouds moving in our direction from the coast. We decided we should get ourselves ready for the 'off' before the rain hit and just as well. Twenty minutes later everyone had to take refuge in their vehicles as sheets of driving torrential rain pounded down. Fortunately, within thirty minutes it had passed and walkers began emerging and continued with their preparations.

Pre-Challenge stretches - or practice celebration?

The atmosphere was congenial, with walkers and drivers from different teams chatting, wishing each other good luck and exchanging opinions on conditions and routes, all underpinned by an air of slight nervous tension. It seemed like there were all kinds who tried the Three Peaks. There were some notable lumps of lads, maybe a bunch of rugby forwards; there was small team of wiry thirty-somethings who looked like they were doing some last minute trained killer exercises; firemen; university teams; DIY store managers; families; and all age groups from maybe ten to seventy.

One Welsh guy told us that a party he had met earlier that day had started

Preparations at Achintee

at **Snowdon** and finished on the **Ben**, but only after seven hours and out of time as they chose to do it by the **Carn Mor Dearg arê te**. Fantastically ambitious and either brave or foolhardy - I don't know which.

Turn left for Ben Nevis

Actually, both Alec and I felt surprisingly nervous as the time crept closer to four o' clock. We both used the toilets of the **Ben Nevis Inn** at least twice. We spent a few moments posing for photographs with Geoff and Mark, made some last minute adjustments to our kit and then all of a sudden it was time to go. Several other teams started at the same time and there was a rush forward.

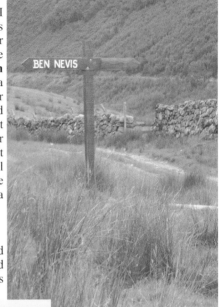
Turn left for Ben Nevis

Almost immediately I had to admit to myself that I did not feel strong, with legs

About to disappear from view .... maybe forever

that felt more than a little rubbery. I gritted my teeth and pushed hard. I was in front, Alec following maybe five metres behind, keeping pace fine.

After a couple of minutes we topped the first rise, about to disappear from the view of Geoff and Mark. We turned and waved. When we later viewed this scene on the camcorder, we heard Geoff's voice murmur, "You know that might be the last time we ever see them ...." followed by Mark chuckling, "You can't say that!"

A 'Last' wave

The youth hostel path comes in from the right

The path was busy, especially as we passed the feeder track coming in from the youth hostel. Hundreds of us snaked our way up the track, with some very large sponsored groups interspersed with smaller parties, all jostling for space.

Soon though, as the ascent started to bite, the ribbon of sweating, panting humanity began to string out. We kept up a good pace, never stopping. This had been our agreed strategy. We would take a maximum of one five-minute break on the top of each mountain, but that was it. Others obviously had a different approach and we passed several groups having drinks and snacks along the way. Some of the leaders of the bigger groups were equipped with walkie-talkies. Probably necessary when you have fifty or more novices in your charge, but it still made them look a bit self-important …. "Roger, Roger, over and out …"

The path was also populated with goodly number of gorgeous young females, presumably belonging to one or other of the university teams. One even wore a thong - not *only* a thong you understand - but with 'whale tale' prominently on display nevertheless. A thong on a mountain, now that's an innovation! Watch out for them in outdoor shops from now on! It certainly proved a welcome distraction, and by the time my mind had drifted back to the condition of my own legs as opposed to theirs I realised that I had walked through my bad patch and they felt strong again. I was sure it would rouse Alec out of any agonies he was suffering too. I checked later - it did.

At the half way point - which is actually well past **Lochan Meall an t-Suidhe**, the so-called **Half Way Lochan**, I did a time check. We were doing well and looked on for an ascent time of two and a half hours. I waited for Alec and told him this. He seemed fine. I turned and marched off.

Amazingly the cloud thinned, some beautiful views opened up, and the mountain was clear all the way to the top. The summit of the **Ben** only gets about sixty clear days each year, and has an average annual rainfall of four metres, so luck was with us.

Almost there: 3 Peakers nearing the summit.

And happily there was only one small patch of snow on the whole route, at the top of the zigzags. (There are perhaps some minor benefits from global warming).

I had lost sight of Alec now and was a little bit anxious, but decided to push on to the top and wait there. Navigating in clear visibility was elementary; just avoid the sheer drops down the gullies.

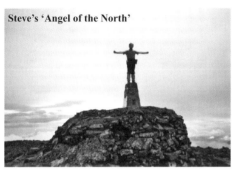
Steve's 'Angel of the North'

I reached the top at 6.23 p.m. It was a great place to be in the early evening. It smelled high, cold and remote. A trained killer who arrived minutes afterwards said, "Your mate's coming," and sure enough Alec arrived at 6.30 p.m. Really good times.

But as soon as he came in sight I could tell all was not well. He was pretty drained. Shortly after I had left him at the half-way point he had experienced severe leg cramps, one of his legs buckling under him, leading to a fall. After five minutes vigorous massage and a long drink he had soldiered on, but at the top he was still in some distress.

Perhaps I shouldn't have asked him if he wanted me to take a photo of him standing on the summit plinth … a definite rebuff! He wolfed down a sandwich and within five minutes of his arrival we headed down.

A less than thrilled look from Alec

I felt pretty good now and steamed on down, but stopped periodically to make sure that Alec was within sight. Then the clouds came down again and for an hour it rained steadily and we had no alternative but to don our waterproofs.

Looking over the edge from the top of the sheer North Face.

Starting the last leg of the descent; the path from Lochan plateau heading back to Glen Nevis.

As Bill Bryson says, "There is no pleasure in walking in waterproofs. There is something deeply dispiriting about the stiff rustle of nylon and the curiously amplified patter of rain on fabric." And you don't even stay dry, especially in mild weather. Yes they keep out the rain, but 'breathable' or not they make you sweat so much that soon you become clammily sodden. And getting in to them is tricky as Bryson describes: "It's a funny thing. I dress myself unaided most mornings, but give me a pair of waterproof trousers to put on and it's as if I've never stood unaided." I knew what he meant as I lurched around the path.

Arriving back at Glen Nevis

I made the car park by 8.33 and Alec rolled in at 8.38. These were excellent times and I was delighted. Alec only cared that for the moment, it was over. He had tripped and fallen full length on the way down too.

"Just pure exertion Geoff,"

he groaned, but later, in the car he admitted that his troubles were probably due to dehydration from our boozy pre-challenge night out. Having said that, it was a dangerous moment, and he told me later he felt seriously bad. Maybe we'd set out too fast. Thankfully he'd had the grit to carry on.

Alec rediscovers his smile

We quickly changed clothing, ready for the next hill and were on our way by nine o' clock. During our absence on the Ben, Geoff and Mark had being preparing our food packs for the next few hours.

This included heating a hot stew for supper, flasks of hot drinks, and rolls for a middle of the night breakfast and ration packs for the next mountain.

We happily tucked into supper now. The sports recovery drinks helped too, I think.

Soon Alec was asleep - which was fine - and slumping sideways onto me, which was not. His propensity to slip readily into a coma and thereafter to snuggle up to whatever body he finds himself beside, regardless of gender, is a worrying one, but can be solved by regular elbowing in the ribs and a good heave. He reluctantly reacted to this treatment by straightening up and leaning back. But ever so gradually his head would subside forward onto his chest. Amid a snuffle and a snort, he'd then lurch upright and the cycle would start again.

We had made thorough preparations to make sleep possible. We had earplugs with us, airline blackout masks, pillows and blankets.

Despite all this I slept not a wink. Instead I texted a progress report home.

By the time we were nearing **Crianlarich** it was virtually dark. We had a very lucky moment as Geoff - following that bloody sat-nav - shot past our turn off for the A82 to **Loch Lomond**. Just at the right moment Alec gave a particularly violent lurch upright, and with a noisy snort awoke from his twitching slumber, saw what was happening and shouted out and saved us. The rest of the journey went smoothly, raining at first but then drying up. There was little traffic down **Loch Lomondside**, no morons in Mini Metros, no caravaners looking for their turn-off, no Norbert Dentressangle juggernauts. And the motorways through **Glasgow** were clear too.

*At our fuel stop at the **Bothwell** services on the M74 we booted up and prepared our kit so far as possible. By the way, for those of you who have drivers who smoke, bear in mind that they will need cigarette breaks. This was something I hadn't factored in, and it extended a couple of driving stops. (As it happened, they made up all of this time and lots more besides.)*

During one of our planning sessions Alec had come up with an additional idea to save time on pee-stops. We could use those hospital type urine bottles and just keep going. This idea was adamantly rejected by Geoff and even more vehemently by Sue, my sister in law, who I think envisaged suspect smells lingering in the car and mouldy patches on the carpet. This despite us promising not to spill the contents! I still think it was a good idea ….

Mark now took over the driving and the pace quickened. With six points already, Geoff was understandably highly conscious about the risk to his licence and his livelihood. Mark quite obviously didn't have the same concern. Before we knew it, we were through **Carlisle** and trekking around the western Lake District.

We had all perked up again now, anticipating the second leg of the challenge. Alec suddenly started writhing in the back, twisting like a felled animal.

"What on earth are you up to back there?" asked Mark.
"Just getting my nuts out," he replied much to my concern. He'd stashed his emergency rations for **Ben Nevis** in his trouser pockets!

Kitting up at Wasdale

Ready to go again …

We made **Wasdale Head** by 1.45 a.m. and were ready for the hills by 2.00 a.m. This was a whole one and a half hours ahead of our schedule and was fantastic. The downside was that it was pitch black dark and would remain so for at least a couple of hours. The cloud was thick so there was no moon, there was no wind and the mist was down to about 300m (1000ft). It wasn't raining, but it was going to be a moist walk.

It seemed we were only the second party to arrive, as there was only one other vehicle there. But within seconds another arrived, no doubt with others hard on its heels. I was tired, not having slept, but the adrenaline was pumping well. Alec seemed rested and ready to go.

We set off up **Lingmell Gill**, which is a faultless guide to the route in the early stages. This route is described by Wainwright as "a tiring and uninteresting grind". It's certainly the steepest ascent of any of the Three Peaks.

Up ahead we saw the lights of the leading group. But even with our head torches it was a struggle to stay on track and we did go a few yards astray where the path crosses the gill.

This was where my specially purchased GPS came into its own, bleeping to indicate a change in direction. I had previously plotted a route on my computer and downloaded it to the GPS and it was this route it was now navigating. I have to admit to being a confirmed map and compass walker, having learnt to navigate in the 70's when no alternative existed. I didn't quite conform to the, "GPS isn't proper navigation" school, but this was the first time I was fully convinced of its worth. It always comes with me on challenge walks now. If you want to know more about GPS, David Brawn's GPS The Easy Way is the book to read.

But even now our navigation difficulties weren't over. Wearing glasses - and I needed to, to read both the GPS and the map card - caused problems as the sweat poured off my forehead and onto the lenses. The problem was soon solved for me. I took them off to wipe them and a lens fell out. With no alternative, I pocketed the bits and carried on. Thank God we had surveyed the route beforehand.

Despite the Stygian blackness and the almost palpable mist, there was no malevolence about the mountain. We never went astray again; however progress was slow because of the tortuous path-finding. But at least we weren't in as much trouble as some others. About ten minutes behind us we had noticed three head torches following us up, with lots of calling going on between the wearers. Then a little later, mystified, we watched as the beams drifted persistently to the right and then disappeared. We never saw them again.

On this mountain, Alec was walking really strongly, positively swinging up the hill. He seemed to have completely recovered from his earlier travails. We reached the top in intense mist after one hour and fifty seven minutes, seventeen minutes outside of our target time, but overall, still substantially ahead of schedule. When we stopped, all was stillness and

"This isn't mist, it's steam." grunted Alec

Misty reflections on the top.
3.58am Saturday

gloom. Now for the second mystery of **Scafell Pike**. We had the summit to ourselves, and no-one had passed us on the way down, so where was the lead group?

But even in dense eerie mist, on the Three Peaks Challenge, you have no time to contemplate ghostly abductions. A handshake and a couple of quick photos and we turned around. It was even difficult route finding on the way down, until ever so gradually it began to get light, although the sky certainly lived up to Bill Bryson's memorable metaphor; "like a pile of wet towels".

.. like a pile of wet towels ..

Now people were streaming up and we began to recognise some Three Peakers from Ben Nevis. No sign of 'The Thong' though - maybe she was after all a figment of an ageing, fevered, dehydrated imagination. Or even worse, **Ben Nevis** had been her last mountain. No hope for **Snowdon** then. Despite this notable absence, the camaraderie on the hillside was enjoyable, with most people saying an encouraging word or two to each other.

I pleased myself by finding and finishing off a half-eaten Snickers bar I had stuffed into my trouser pocket on **Ben Nevis**, albeit now a bit squishy and fluffy. I wasn't sure how many calories fluff contains but I supposed the roughage would do me good.

I was conscious that Alec and I were falling into our familiar pattern - a slow descent - but with Alec trailing behind there was little point in steaming ahead. Then - oh shit - I tripped, couldn't regain my balance and was set to sprawl forwards. At the last second I managed to swerve my body to the left away from the stony path and onto the steep grassy sward alongside. This resulted in a softer landing, but a longer rucksack and arse over head tumble, after which I regained my feet - without losing momentum - followed by several balletic leaps that Darcey Bussell would have been proud of, all culminating in a rather spectacular twenty foot slither. Do bear in mind that at this point there were dozens of people on the path. Yet, after I picked myself up and brushed myself down it seemed that no-one had witnessed my slapstick moment. Except of course Alec who saw me scrambling back to the path - and subsequently has not let me forget my undignified diversion. I was bruised, scuffed, shaken and weak-kneed but thankfully not injured.

We made it down 3 hours 37 minutes after starting. This was a good deal slower than the 3 hours 15 that we had managed in training, but given the navigation difficulties, perhaps not too bad. I was just glad to be down.

Geoff and Mark were curled up, dozing in the cosy car, radio issuing

A grateful return to Wasdale - minus specs

gentle music. Here's a tip for those readers who might one day do support: please at least *try* to give the impression that it's purgatory for you too.

"That mountain was not good to me," I moaned to anyone who would listen. No one paid much attention, but the phrase was soon taken up as a piss-take by Alec, and it has come back to haunt me since.

"That mountain was not good to me"

I'd expected Alec to be pretty down in the mouth too, but actually he was annoyingly chipper, saying he'd found it much easier than expected. I forbore to point out that as I had been slower in ascent because of the difficult route finding, he had had a slower and therefore easier trek on the mountain.

At no point had his renewed vigour tempted him to take the lead ... Still, it was good that his self confidence had returned.

In contrast with a few hours previously, every available car parking space had been taken; cars, vans, minibuses everywhere, many of which we recognised from Ben Nevis. Geoff and Mark, who had been chatting to the other support teams, told us of one group travelling in two minibuses. It was only on the way from **Fort William** to **Wasdale** that they discovered that their hired vehicles were speed-governed to a maximum of 62 mph. As a result they were over an hour late arriving at **Scafell Pike**. Disaster!

I never realised it at the time, but minibuses have different speed limits from cars anyway; 50 on a single carriageway, 60 on a dual carriageway and 70 on a motorway. This could have a major impact on a schedule as all the way from **Fort William** *to the* **Erskine Bridge** *is single carriageway.*

As for us, we piled into our car and with Mark at the wheel, followed twenty miles of single track roads towards **Duddon Bridge** and the main road to the **M6** south. At six in the morning the roads were empty, so despite the twists, turns, ups and downs of the route we made good time. Once again our rations had been prepared, so we breakfasted and then tried to sleep again. Because of their supporter duties, Mark and Geoff had not had any sleep so far. But finally, on the **M6** I drifted off. I woke after only forty-five minutes, but amazingly I felt totally refreshed. We swapped drivers at an **M6** services and carried on. Everyone's spirits were high now. With only one mountain to go we had a comfortable time cushion and were optimistic for success. We made a phone call home and updated our families - and were warned not to get complacent or cocky! Even the sat-nav behaved itself on this stretch of our journey, guiding us faultlessly to **Pen y Pass** by 10.15am.

As feared, the car park was full. We recognised the attendant from our training session, as he peremptorily waved us on, enjoying his job too much.

Ready for mountain number three ...

With nowhere to pull over even for a few minutes, we drove another mile down the pass to the **Pen y Gwyrd Hotel**. There we kitted ourselves up and drove back up to **Pen y Pass** where Geoff and Mark dropped us off. We started mountain number three at 10.39, one hour and twenty one minutes ahead of schedule.

In over thirty years of fellwalking we had never experienced such a busy mountain. Mostly people were just strolling, which of course did us no favours. We took the **Pyg Track** and made reasonable progress at first. The weather was of the classic sunshine and showers type and soon we were walking in waterproofs again. The slow pace of many of the day trippers would normally be merely irksome, now it was infuriating. Especially where the path narrowed and took to rocky staircases, lengthy queues formed. And some of the day trippers were massive. There was definitely a surfeit of overripe human flesh. Women with fleshy arms, midriff-baring tops and shorts abounded, looking remarkably like cartoon hippos in shrunken clothes. Thank God there were no thong wearers here. And just in case you think that is a sexist observation, during a brief sunny spell I then found myself walking behind the biggest backside I've ever seen on a mountain and experienced my own personal solar eclipse. As I passed by, I noticed that it was nicely counter-balanced by a bulging, over-hanging beer gut.

While Alec and I were on this third mountain, Mark and Geoff had no more supporting duties to fulfil and took the opportunity to snatch a couple of hours of well deserved sleep in the car, their first in over thirty hours.

On the **Pyg Track** there were still a few familiar faces from **Ben Nevis** and **Scafell Pike**, but well scattered now. I passed one mixed gender group of five, all wearing sponsorship T-shirts and overheard the following conversation.

"Well as far as I'm concerned, *we* are the team, not the rest of those layabouts on the bus. They think it's a joke, no-one's committed, some of them have hardly trained and they've held us back ..."

The conversation trailed away as I moved past, but it started me thinking about the difficulties of succeeding at such a challenge as part of a big group of twenty, thirty, fifty or more. With such numbers to deal with, and the whole spectrum of personality, attitudes, commitment levels, fitness levels and hill walking experience - or inexperience - the chances of something going awry are multiplied enormously. The group moves at the pace of the slowest.

Apparently - so I learned afterwards from a friend who had taken part in just such a fundraising walk - when walking with some big charity groups, the organisers position stewards at various elevations on each of the mountains. If a participant gets a 'hand on the shoulder' from one of them, it means they are out of time and they must turn around immediately even if the summit is in sight - and head back to the bus. By this method they try to keep to the schedule. But imagine the strained atmosphere on the bus after the first and second mountains. Some walkers will be cock-a-hoop and excited about the rest of the expedition. The failures must be resigned or morose. And on the hill, even if energetic splinter groups walk at their own pace, they still have to wait for stragglers at the bus. The whole exercise is also highly dependent upon the quality of leadership provided by the organisers.

On other charity events, each team is responsible for its own transport, equipment and navigation. The charity provides first-aid cover and safety marshalls on the mountains, but teams take part at their own risk. They wear the charity's T-shirt, turn up at the allotted time, but they're then responsible for their own destiny. This seems much closer to the real spirit of hill walking, acting with some independence rather than being shepherded along. The old proverb, 'he travels fastest who travels alone,' certainly applies. In my view, the fastest walking team is a team of one. I'm astonished that so many of those who take part in huge charity groups succeed in a twenty-four hour challenge. Credit is due.

At **Achintee**, Alec and I had chatted to a walker from another group (of five). This was to be a second attempt by him on the Three Peaks having failed the first time because the group of nine experienced walkers he was with twelve months ago did such a great time on the **Ben** and subsequently **Scafell Pike**, that they decided - by a majority vote apparently - that they could take an hour out for a sit down meal at an **M6** Services. It seems hubris affects fell walkers too. The meal drifted on for an hour and twenty minutes. Back on the road again they hit traffic problems, were late arriving at **Snowdon**, and none of them managed to come in under twenty-four hours. He was still spitting blood a year later.

Even in smaller groups like ours, personality factors can cause havoc. Alec, Geoff and I were friends before the event a huge advantage. But we are all very different characters. Alec is a people person - albeit occasionally an undiplomatic one - always happy to spend time getting to know people and their business, an extrovert and an energetic activist who is always pleased to be along for the ride. Geoff is also an extrovert in that he probably prefers to be around people; however he is also a highly structured and organised person with tendencies to perfection. This is balanced by being so laid back that nothing gets done in a hurry. To misquote Pete McCarthy, if you're waiting for Geoff, "there's just time to shave, grow more stubble and shave again". I'm the pushy one, despite being more introverted than the other two. With a tendency to take charge and an inclination for straight talking, I try to make things happen and quickly - which I think can be irritating for others sometimes. Nah … Perhaps the one common characteristic between the three of us is a sense of humour and the willingness to laugh at ourselves and take the piss out of each other.

Mark was really the unknown quantity in our team. As it happened, everything panned out well, but I recognised from the beginning that we were taking a risk. Geoff knew Mark from work, but before the challenge I had met him for only fifteen minutes, and Alec not at all. Mark quietly accommodated all our foibles and absolutely delivered the goods. But it could have been quite different.

Steve 'ferreting'

And there were indeed some moments of minor tension during our expedition; between Geoff and I after he had spent ages carefully re-packing the kit in the boot and I arrived fresh off the hills and started ferreting (as he called it) for some kit that I believed should have been on the top; and when Alec murmured to me that Geoff was driving too slowly, it fell to me to ask him to speed up.

Wordlessly, he eased his foot down … And at the bottom of **Scafell Pike**, Alec and I put each other's noses out of joint briefly when spilling out our experiences. None of this really mattered and nothing got blown out of proportion because we knew each other well enough. That and the fact that we were all committed, and very clear about our roles, responsibilities and the groundrules.

We were lucky with Mark. He has since become a friend and has joined us on other forays in the hills. But I'd wager that many Three Peak challenges have failed because of poor team fit.

Anyway, getting back to **Snowdon**, the cloud base was well down the mountain so the summit ridge was obscured. The climb seemed much longer as a result, and tougher, but I guess this was also a function of tired limbs. Indeed, almost walking in tandem with us were three generations of a family; boy, girl, father and granddad. This was all very pleasant

The last few steps of the ascent

except that white haired granddad kept leapfrogging past us and eventually disappeared upwards, only to pass us again on his way back down.

Most British mountains seem to have a pleasing capacity to absorb newcomers to the hills, but **Snowdon** had just been overwhelmed. At the **Pigtop Pillar** a huge crowd of day trippers were hanging around. Many of them were smoking out of the corner of their mouths. A few were taking swigs from beer cans. One or two multi-skilled individuals were doing both. Most no doubt had come up on the railway, which during the rebuilding work at the summit station, terminated at **Clogwyn**, one stop before. I'm with Wainwright on this one. Encountering humanity en masse on the hills is generally a disagreeable experience, and if I could have avoided this slovenly mob, I would have.

Third peak 'summitted' 12.54p.m. Saturday

The next best thing was to blaze a trail through them and soldier on to the summit, which itself was draped with another blanket of human flotsam. We clambered through them to the top, 1 hour 55 minutes after starting.

The hard work was done now; all we had to do was to stay safe and continue to put one foot in front of the other.

The standing stone at the junction of the Pyg and Miners' tracks

Our descent was slow though, impeded even more frequently by more members of the Hefty Hikers Club that were picking their sloth-like way down the rocky staircase accompanied by grunts of exertion and squeaks of anxiety.

Suppressing an urge to shriek - or even trip a few of them up - I shuffled on. One of them had a dog in tow that looked just as thuggish as its shaven-headed master. It was persistently trying to pee on any vertical surface it could find and in so doing stretching its extendable lead across the path like a trip wire. The owner was oblivious to looks of visceral hatred from ascenders and descenders alike but no-one, including me, was going to say anything. I decided after all that my tripping urge might not be terribly wise.

From the **Pigtop Pillar** to the junction with the **Miners' Track** we made excruciatingly slow time. Another standing stone marks the bifurcation of the paths. Here we turned down to the right, and immediately our progress became speedier. After the final steep descent, we only had three more miles of easy, gently declining path. For the first time in our endeavour we chatted as we walked.

We felt good now; tired but fully confident we had it licked. We strolled. And then, with two miles to go, we realised that if we got a move on we could come in at under twenty two and a half hours. So we piled it on again, as best we could. With a mile to go, it still looked possible. Then, as we rounded a bend, we encountered four young guys wearing Three Peaks T shirts, running *up* the mountain. We cheered them on. We discovered later that they belonged to the team travelling in the speed limited mini buses and had only just arrived at **Pen y Pass**. Most of the group had given up and stayed in the bus, but these few guys decided to go for broke. I hope they made it.

And we came in together at 2.29 p.m. on Saturday 23 June 2007, completing **Snowdon** in three hours and fifty minutes and the whole challenge in twenty two hours and twenty nine minutes. We thought that wasn't too bad for two old boys …

"Well, we knocked the bastard off."

Sir Edmund Hillary, mountaineer, about Everest.

So, we headed to the **Pen y Gwyrd** bar to celebrate, enjoyed a couple of pints and then went on to our hotel, **Cobdens** at **Capel Curig**. This is a great example of an old fashioned unponced-up Welsh hostelry. Okay, it probably hadn't been refurbished since the eighties and it did have those carpets with the kind of patterns you only otherwise see after you've rubbed your eyes too hard, but it was clean, warm, welcoming and good value.

The back bar has been built right up against a rock outcrop and it has something of the dank atmosphere of a cave, with fern fronds sprouting from crevices in the stone. Shrek would feel at home here, but like Shrek's swamp it has a convivial homely ambience.

The 'Scottish' pool team

That afternoon, the English pool team exacted their revenge. Geoff would not give in until the scores were 10 for England and 9 for Scotland. I thought this was taking unfair advantage of our exhaustion and a betrayal of our team ethos.

Later, after taking turns to ring our respective baths with 24-hours worth of accumulated sweat and muck from three different countries, we met for dinner.

It made a pleasant change to sit at a table rather than eating in the back of

the car or on the hoof.

Alec and I had previously decided we would present Mark and Geoff with a memento to mark our appreciation for all their support. We had prepared and framed tongue-in-cheek 'certificates of achievement' and also had an engraved beer tankard for each of them. But before we gave them out, we had a special presentation to make. Alec had managed to acquire two hospital urine bottles which we had gift wrapped. With a flourish and a good deal of insincere thanks, he now presented them. They unwrapped them with anticipation.

"Bastards!" mouthed Geoff when he saw what was inside.

Then we presented the real gifts. In their turn, and to our surprise, Geoff and Mark presented us with Three Peaks logo-ed polo shirts to mark our achievement.

We had a slap up three course meal and a good laugh, but no-one lasted beyond 10 p.m. before heading for bed. Sleep deprivation and the potent effects of real ale on the exhausted human body won in the end.

Eleven REFLECTIONS

"Whether you believe you can, or whether you believe you can't, you're absolutely right."

Henry Ford, businessman

The next morning (in presentation shirts). Stiff, tired and relieved.

In retrospect we got many more things right than we got wrong.

What would we change? Well, we'd not drink so much before the off! We'd start later at **Ben Nevis**, say 5.30 p.m. instead of 4.00 p.m. so that we would get to **Scafell Pike** as it gets light. We'd kit up for **Snowdon** at the service station at the A55/A5 junction so that we could just leap out of the car at **Pen y Pass**. We'd change the route up **Snowdon** to the **Miners' Track**. We wouldn't take so much food. We'd skip the **Clachaig Inn**. We'd bury the sat-nav so Geoff couldn't find it. And that's about it.

A couple of months later, when next travelling up **Loch Lomondside**, Alec called in at the tearoom we'd stopped at and spoke to the proprietor. Looking him straight in the eye she said,

"I knew you'd make it. I'm never wrong."

If only we'd known! But actually, we had never really contemplated failure. We'd always visualised success and talked often about our end of challenge celebrations. The power of visualisation is immense.

Overall, we were moderately pleased with our performance. But we recognised that our times were by no means exceptional. We felt that with a longer training period we could have done better. Indeed, we have since climbed all three mountains again   separately and taken a significant amount off our best times.

Upon reflection, the National Three Peaks Challenge has had a lasting impact upon us for the better. Both of us have continued with our daily four-mile training walk. This has had a beneficial effect upon our health. My weight, cholesterol level, blood pressure and resting pulse rate have all come down (although mysteriously there has been no effect on my liver function).

It has rekindled our enthusiasm for fellwalking and we have made many more forays to the hills since the challenge.

On one of these, Geoff and Mark joined us. This was an interesting introductory experience for Mark. We tackled **Great Gable** and having made it to the top problem free, we went slightly astray when leaving the summit and ended up descending the steep scree slope to **Beck Head** at the col between **Great Gable** and **Kirk Fell**. This was his first encounter with scree and he didn't like it one little bit. His strategy was to crouch down on the stones and use his backside to brake his downward slither. After about half an hour he got to the bottom, with his trousers soaking wet, muddied up from ankles to waist, but enormously relieved.

"That's the scariest thing I've ever done," he said.
"Never mind that," said Alec, "You must have half the stones off the hillside up your arse."

A few days later we that heard Mark had been taken into hospital with severe stomach pains. It turned out to be gall stones. When I told Alec he said,

"I told you it was stones up his arse.'"

Happily, Mark made a full recovery.

Despite this incident, Mark has now taken up hill walking. Even Geoff occasionally raises his eyes to the peaks and takes a leisurely stroll in their direction. It has strengthened the friendship between the four of us.

And Alec and I have caught the achievement bug again. By August we had decided that we would tackle the English Three-thousanders as our challenge for the following year. This entails walking 34 continuous miles (54 kms) and climbing almost 12,000 feet (3600m) in under 24 hours. It will be the toughest thing we've attempted. We've been in training since October and have had our fair share of adventures in so doing. Support this time will be provided by Alec's daughter Lynsey and her partner Neill, because, get this; Mark and Geoff are going to join us for the beginning of the challenge. Never say never …

Alec and I are already speculating about a challenge for a return fixture for the N3P. But this time we'd do it for charity. So if you tackle it then, watch out for us and say hello. Alec will be the one at the side of the path with cramp and I'll be doing *grand jetés* across the hillside.

Something worth celebrating!

Remember - it's the Team that counts.

"Knowledge is understanding that a tomato is a fruit. Wisdom is not putting it in a fruit salad."

John Walkley, coach, trainer.

So based upon our own experiences, here are our suggestions for what to do and not to do. We hope it helps.

We suggest you:-

- use walking poles,

- take drinks from a drinks bladder,

- create laminated route cards rather than taking a full map, but remember to mark coordinate lines,

- make sure that all walkers can navigate,

- use a mix of daily walking and periodic long mountain outings to get fit,

- get together with your fellow team members for training as often as possible. You can't build a team remotely,

- take a GPS if you have one, loaded with the relevant tracks and waypoints. Take lots of extra batteries and change them before each mountain,

- pack your backpacks carefully so you have ready access to items you're likely to need,

- make sure you have a big enough vehicle so walkers have sufficient space to sleep comfortably; we had a Mondeo and it was only just big enough for the four of us,

- reconnoitre all the mountains beforehand if you can; if you have to miss one, don't make it **Scafell Pike**,

- undertake a fitness trial early on, to establish your 'training gap',

- have at least one driver, preferably two,

- ask your drivers to provide hot food and drinks,

- take ear plugs and blindfold masks for sleeping in the car,

- anticipate a slow walk on **Snowdon**, due to overcrowding - unless you do it in the middle of the night,

- take some toilet tissue with you on the hills, wrapped in a plastic bag. Sometimes your digestive system springs surprises on you. But if needs must, choose your spot with consideration,

- use a Rohan cape for waterproof wear. This was a solution we discovered after the event. They're easy to put on and well ventilated. They cost about £60,

- early on, agree who will be the team leader,

- agree the team's ground-rules and give each other permission to hold each other to them,

- choose interesting walks in their own right for your training outings,

- undertake at least one night-time hill walk as part of your training, ideally, on the peak you intend to tackle in the dark,

- acknowledge up front with your fellow team members that there are likely to be tensions, but that no proper fallouts are allowed!

- visualise success and keep it in your head. The mental picture of the moment of completion is worth an extra three months of training,

- kit up before you reach **Snowdon** so you can make a quick exit at **Pen y Pass**,

- record the event on video if you have a camcorder. It brings it all flooding back and is a good laugh.

We would advise you *not* to:-

- admit any new members to your team without knowing them well,

- try to drive yourself as well as doing the challenge,

- take breaks on the mountains for food or drinks,

- use any equipment which you have not previously trialed (especially sat-nav),

- drink too much the night before the challenge!

- ease off if you're ahead of schedule,

- hire a vehicle without checking speed limits and checking if it's governed,

- drive straight back home after the event. You'll all be tired and it's great to take some time to celebrate and relax, so stay over if you can,

- just follow your leader. It's more fun if you take responsibility for your own success,

- ignore it if one of your team is feeling down. It's normal to have lows as well as highs during the months of preparation, so be prepared to help each other out of them.

Chronological Plan for the Three Peaks Challenge

Dates:-	Thursday 21 - Sunday 24 June
Phase of the moon:-	Quarter-moon
Sunset:-	22.23
Sunrise:-	04.30

Sat Nav postcodes:-

Achintee Car Park	PH33 6TE
Wasdale Head National Trust Campsite	CA20 1EX
Pen y Pass	LL55 4NY

Driving distance:- (from/to **Darlington**)	1120 miles
Petrol contribution by Steve & Alec:-	£60 each

GROUND RULES

- All monies payable will be made to Steve by 2 June 07. An allowance of £20 per head for the final dinner will be included for each participant. (Any under/overspend will be adjusted on Sunday morning). Steve will settle the hotel bill, and will forward the fuel allowance to Geoff by cheque in ample time before the event.

- Walkers will walk together (ish!) on the mountains. In particular, both walkers will approach and leave the summit area of **Ben Nevis** together. Should one walker become injured on a mountain and the other wishes to continue, then both walkers will return to the car together. Thereafter, the expedition will proceed as planned, with the remaining walker attempting the challenge. Should one walker become injured on the final mountain (**Snowdon**), if the injured walker is safe and is able to get off the mountain alone, the remaining walker will continue with the challenge. If either or both walkers fail in the challenge, a new date will be set to repeat the challenge during 2007.

- Alec has chosen not to walk with a belly bag, Steve will do so. Whatever the case, walkers must be properly organised, so that proper clothing is worn at the beginning of each mountain and items are stowed in appropriate pockets for each walk, *so that it is not necessary to stop to search for items in backpacks*.

- Walkers will undertake at least 3 minutes of warm up/down stretches at the beginning and end of each ascent (see separate stretch guide).
- At the *first suspicion* of the development of a blister, walkers will

stop to apply the appropriate treatment.

- Walkers will ***not*** stop for meal or drink breaks on the mountains, but will eat and drink on the move. Drinks will be taken from platypuses.

- No more than 5 minutes will be spent on the summit of each mountain, during which time photos will be taken. Geoff will pass on progress texts to Chris & Ve as each mountain is descended (Down 1, Down 2, Down 3)

- Drivers are responsible for basic vehicle checks: oil, water, washer bottle etc. Geoff to fuel up before the start. One overnight bag per person is permitted, with the minimum items allowed (toiletries & underwear) as space will be very tight.

- Drivers commit to being at the agreed spot and ready to drive, the moment the walkers arrive back at the rendezvous, with all provisions prepared and equipment packed away. When possible, walkers descending mountains will phone the drivers 40 minutes before ETA . (This will not be possible at **Wasdale** where there is no mobile phone signal). Drivers will agree between themselves when to change over during journeys. These should be at times which will cause minimum delay to the expedition. Drivers should have a plentiful supply of ready change for bridge or tunnel tolls.

- A video diary of the event will be made. Drivers will be responsible for recording the walkers' departures and arrivals, without the need for repeat takes. Any proceeds from 'You've Been Framed' will be split between all parties. Steve will copy the film onto a video cassette for each participant after the event.

- Fun will be had by all, and the piss will be taken at every opportunity.

GETTING TOGETHER THURSDAY 21/6

Steve, Chris & Nicole drive to **Darlington**. Depart 0900 arrive 1300 - 1330
Mark to meet with Geoff & Steve at Geoff's place at 1400
Depart **Darlington** by 1500 arriving at **Dumfries** by 1730
Geoff & Steve to check traffic/roadworks websites before departure:

www.trafficscotland.org
www.highways.gov.uk/trafficinfo
www.rac.co.uk/web/trafficnews/incidents

Also check mountain weather sites/numbers:-

www.mwis.org.uk (Ben Nevis)
Weatherline 0870 055 0575 **(Scafell Pike)**
www.metoffice.gov.uk/outdoor/mountainsafety/snowdonia.html
(Snowdon)

ACCOMMODATION

Thursday night at an excellent and remarkably cheap B & B (Alec's place)

SCHEDULE FRIDAY 22/6

- Depart **Dumfries** by 0900
- Arrive at **Fort William** (**Achintee** car park) by 1500 on Friday having had lunch on the way at the **Clachaig Inn**, **Glen Coe**.
- Steve & Alec start walking at 1600

WALKERS'ASCENT NOTES

Ben Nevis. 4347 ft of ascent. Total time: 5 hours 30. Target time back at base 2130.

- start and finish at the **Achintee Visitor Centre** car park, 140º
- cross river and ascend to join path ascending SE, 140º
- continue to junction of path from Youth Hostel, 140º
- ascend SE turning NE on path on LHS above **Red Burn**, 45º
- at first zig (to left) bearing 269º then zag at 58º above **Lochan Meall an t-Suidhe**
    - ascend S (160º) then ESE 50º on zig-zag path on boulder strewn slopes. Where path straightens, ascend just S of E towards ruin (Do not navigate direct to summit) 111º
- from ruins head NNE to summit, 50º
- reverse route to return

NAVIGATING OFF THE SUMMIT

There is likely to be thick mist on the top, as the mountain only has 60 clear days each year. On the north side of the summit is the precipitous north face and to the south, the ground drops away steeply to **Coire Eoghainn** and **Five Finger Gully**. When descending from the summit trig point it is essential to navigate well clear of **Gardyloo Gully** (150 metres on a grid bearing of 231º) before turning to a grid bearing of 282º.

    Summit:- 3 hours 15 mins
    Car park:- 5 hours 30 mins

DRIVERS'ACTIVITIES 1600 - 2130

Video walkers departure (& some of own activities during the waiting period)

1900 - 2000
- Heat up broth & decant into labeled flasks for each walker.
- Make tea (for Steve, strong, only a drop of milk, no sugar), & coffee (for Alec, milk, no sugar) & put into labeled flasks.
- Make up meal packs for each walker of 2 x buttered rolls & custard pot.

- Fill small bottle of fruit juice for each walker.
- Fill small bottle (330ml) of recovery drink for each walker (1 sachet per bottle).
- Sort out yourselves with grub & drink as you wish.
- Prepare mountain drinks in container (50/50 juice/water) for next mountain.
- Wash up pots, pans & utensils.
- Video walkers' return.
- Be ready to leave by 2045 (just in case of a miracle time by walkers!)

ROUTE: FRIDAY NIGHT / SATURDAY MORNING

Fort William to **Wasdale** (5.5 hours or less)
Depart by 2200 latest.   Arrive **Wasdale** 0330 latest

From **Ben Nevis** head back towards **Fort William** but avoid the town centre by taking the bypass (straight over at the mini roundabout) and then head south on the **A82**, passing **Corran Ferry**, and crossing the **Ballachullish Bridge**, after which you turn left still on the **A82** bypassing **Glencoe** village to the left and following the main road up the pass and across **Rannoch Moor**. Then on through **Bridge of Orchy** and **Tyndrum** to **Crianlarich**. Turn right, continuing on the **A82** down the side of **Loch Lomond** - over the **Erskine Bridge**, picking up the **M8** through **Glasgow**, joining the **M74** south at **junction 22**.

Once on the **M74** we'll probably need a fuel and toilet stop. **Bothwell** services is the first one, but there are good services further on at **Gretna** if we want to get more miles under our belts. Then follow the **M74** all the way to the **M6**. At **junction 44** of the **M6** take the **A7** into **Carlisle**. At around midnight the roads are quiet. From **Carlisle** town centre, follow signs for the **A595** heading towards **Workington** and then **Whitehaven**. At **Thursby** roundabout take the second left to continue on the **A595** through **Mealsgate** and **Bothel**, to meet the **A66** outside of **Cockermouth**. Turn right onto the **A66** for a short distance, before following signs again for the **A595** toward **Whitehaven**. As you approach **Whitehaven**, keep left to avoid the town centre, staying on the **A595**. Carry on through **Egremont**, **Calderbridge** and **Ponsonby**. Shortly afterwards take a left turning signposted to **Gosforth**. Head into the village, then at the main junction turn left towards **Wasdale**. Bear next left and continue to a junction where you should bear right, up a very steep road. Carry on through **Nether Wasdale** and turn left at the next junction, - signposted for **Wasdale Head**.

Wast Water will soon appear on your right. Continue over several humpback bridges and about a mile before **Wasdale Head** turn right at the **National Trust Campsite**. Follow this track through the car park until it ends at the beginning of a footpath. Park here. This may not be possible as the car park is often closed on summer nights from 8.30 p.m. until 7.30 a.m. to prevent disturbance to the camp site. In which case, park at the roadside lay-by and as soon as the gate opens move to the above position.

WALKERS' ASCENT NOTES

Scafell Pike 3000 ft of ascent / total time: 3 hours 30 mins

- start and finish at end of National Trust Campsite car park. (**Brackenclose**)
- follow **Lingmell Gill** up LHS on 82° until crossing of ford over gill
- then bearing 97° to **Hollow Stones** then 62° to **Lingmell Col**
- at col turn right up hill on 163°
- to descend from summit follow bearing 330°

Timings:

Big cairn after path diverges	50
Rectangular rock	1.15
Summit	2.00
Car park	3.30

DRIVERS' ACTIVITIES

Video walkers departure (& some of own activities during the waiting period)

2 hours after departure:

- Mix beans, bacon & sausage, heat well and long, adding water as necessary and stirring to stop burning and then decant into labeled flasks for each walker.
- Make tea (for Steve, strong, only a drop of milk, no sugar), & coffee (for Alec, milk, no sugar) & put into labeled flasks.
- Make up meal packs for each walker of 2 x buttered rolls.
- Fill small bottle of fruit juice for each walker.
- Fill small bottle (330ml) of recovery drink for each walker (1 sachet per bottle).
- Sort out yourselves with grub & drink as you wish.
- Prepare mountain drinks in container (50/50 juice/water) for next mountain.
- Wash up pots, pans & utensils.
- Video walkers' return.
- Be ready to leave by 3 hours after departure (just in case of miracle time by walkers).

ROUTE: SATURDAY MORNING

Wasdale to **Snowdon** (4.5 hours or less)

Depart by 0730 latest. Arrive **Snowdon** 1200 latest.

Head back from **Wasdale** to **Nether Wasdale** and turn left at the junction signposted for **Santon Bridge**. At **Santon Bridge** follow signs for **Eskdale Green**. At the end of **Eskdale Green** village turn right for **Ulpha**, following a twisty minor road to meet the main **A595** near **Duddon Bridge**. Turn left onto the **A595**. At **Grizebeck**, bear left onto the **A5092**. Follow to this to **Greenodd** where you turn left onto the **A590**, which will take you all the way to the **M6**.

Join the **M6** at **junction 36** and head south all the way to **junction 20**. This is the **M6/M56** intersection. Follow the **M56** signposted 'North Wales and Chester' and carry on all the way to the end of the **M56** which ends at a large roundabout - turn left onto the **A5117**. Then it's straight over at the next roundabout still on the **A5117**. At traffic lights, bear left staying on the dual carriageway, which now becomes the **A550 Queensferry**. Stay on this dual carriageway which becomes the **A494** and then the **A55** - following signs for **Conwy** or **Bangor**. The coast road has varying speed limits. Speed cameras are concentrated around **Conwy** and **Colwyn Bay**. This is a fast piece of road where you can make good time.

The **A55** bypasses **Conwy**, after which you should follow signs for **Bangor**, until you reach the **A5** turn off. Take this sliproad and turn left at the roundabout towards **Bethesda**, then immediately right, past a petrol station onto the **A4244**. At the next roundabout, turn left still on the **A4244**, following signs for **Llanberis**. At the T junction with the **A4086** turn left. Carry on along the main road which bypasses **Llanberis** centre on the right. Follow the road to the summit of **Pen-y-Pass** (four miles further on) and turn right into the turning area of the car park. If possible - which is unlikely, park here. If not, drop off walkers, and return to **Llanberis**. Return to **Pen y Pass** three and a half hours later to pick them up, hopefully triumphant.

WALKERS' ASCENT NOTES: SNOWDON

Start at **Pen y Pass** car park.
Take **Pyg Track**. Return by **Miners' Track**, finishing at the **Pen Y Pass** car park.

Total time	3 hours 30mins
Summit	2.00
Car park	3.30

DRIVERS' ACTIVITIES

- video walkers departure & some of own activities during the waiting period
- 3 hours after departure: prepare chilled champagne for celebration when conquering heroes return.
- video walkers return
- all celebrate with champagne!

ACCOMMODATION

Saturday night at **Cobdens Hotel**, **Capel Curig** LL24 0EE 01690 720243 (Twin rooms)

TRAVEL BACK FROM WALES

- Depart hotel by 1015,
- Drop Steve off at **Crewe** station by 1245 for train back to

Charlbury. (Dep 1310 Arr. 1603),

- Drop Addie off at hotel at **Penrith** roundabout by 1515, for collection.

MEALS

Friday 1600	On hill		Isotonic drinks or 50/50 juice/water Chocolate & flapjack bars Creatine & Carbohydrate Tablets Carbo gel 1 x sandwiches for summit. Banana Nuts & raisins (bagged up)
Friday 2200	In car		Homemade broth/stew, with rolls. Flasks Custard pot Fruit juice
Sat	0230	In car	Sandwiches, pasties Hot tea/coffee
Sat	0330	On hill	Isotonic drinks or 50/50 juice/water Chocolate & flapjack bars Creatine & Carbohydrate Tablets Carbo gel 1 x sandwiches for summit. Banana Nuts & raisins (bagged up)
Sat	0730	In car	Beans, sausage & bacon with rolls Flasks Fruit juice
Sat	1030	In car	Sandwiches, pasties Hot tea/coffee
Sat	1200	On hill	Isotonic drinks or 50/50 juice/water Chocolate & flapjack bars Creatine & Carbohydrate Tablets Carbo gel 1 x sandwiches for summit Banana Nuts & raisins (bagged up)
Fridge food			Filled rolls x 24 Frozen stew Frozen sausage & bacon (for adding to beans) Pasties x 8 Milk

		Fruit juice
Food store		Beans (3 tins)
		Buttered Rolls x 18
		Tea
		Coffee
		Chocolate bars
		Nuts & raisins
		Muesli bars
		Creatine & Carbohydrate Tablets
		Apples
		Bananas
		Salt
		Pepper
Equipment	**In car**	Torch for navigating in car
		Sat Nav (if Geoff can borrow)
		Flashlight
		Head-torches x 2
		Water container for car
		Flasks x 7
		Camping stoves x 2
		Camping pots & kettle
		Small camping table
		Deck chairs x 2
		Nylon canopy & poles
		Plastic jug
		Gas canisters
		Matches
		Stove Windshield
		Toilet roll & kitchen roll
		Tea towel
		Fridge
		Pillows x 3
		Car blankets x 3
		Face cloths (for cleaning up in car)
		Wet wipes
		Paper food dishes
		Spoons (plastic)
		Forks
		Knives
		2 x changes of spare clothes (socks, underwear, T shirts, etc)
		Plastic bags (lots of)
		Bin bags for wet clothes
		Airline masks x 4
		Personal luggage for overnights inc. toilet bags
		Alarm clock
		Sellotape
		String

First aid kit.
Compete
Vaseline
Stapler
Camping table
Nylon canopy
Midge repellent
Moleskin for blisters
Midge repellent
Camcorder
Washing up liquid
Washing up sponge/scourer
Plastic disposable cups

On the hill

Day pack
Bivvy bag
Compass
GPS
Whistle
Route cards
Waterproof (if rain forecast)
Fleece
Sandwich
Drinks in platypuses
Lucozade Carbo Gel
Camera
Lucozade Tablets

RESPONSIBILITIES (WHO WILL PROVIDE WHAT)

(St = Steve Ch = Chris Al = Alec Ve is Ve Ma = Mark Ge = Geoff Sue is Sue)

ITEM	St & Ch	Al & Ve	Ma	Ge & Sue
IN CAR				
Torch for navigating				x
Flashlight				x
Head torches	x	x		
Water container for car	x			
2nd water container for juice/water mix	x			
Flasks	x2	x2	x1	x2
Camping stoves (gas)		x2		
Stove windshield	x			
Camping pots & kettle		x		
Kitchen roll		x		
Tea Towel				x
Plastic jug for decanting into flasks				x
Toilet roll		x		
Cardboard boxes for separating gear in car				x
Fridge	x			
Pillows x 2				x
Blankets x 2		x		
Face cloths	x	x	x	x
Hand towel	x	x	x	x
Spray deodorant (car)		x		
Wet wipes	x			
Cool bag for buttered rolls etc		x		
Polystyrene food dishes				x
Spoons (plastic)	x			
Knives (plastic)	x			
Forks (plastic)	x			
Sticky labels for gear	x			
Plastic disposable cups (8)	x			
Matches	x			
Lighters			x	x
Freezer bags for sandwiches & food on hills		x		

RESPONSIBILITIES(WHO WILL PROVIDE WHAT)

ITEM	St & Ch	Al & Ve	Ma	Ge & Sue
2 x changes of clothes	x	x		
Personal luggage	x	x	x	x
Plastic carrier bags (12)				x
Bin bags (roll of)				x
Airline masks x 4	x			
Alarm clock				x
String	x			
Stapler	x			
Sellotape	x			
Midge repellent	x	x		
First aid kit for car	x			
Vaseline		x		
Moleskin for blisters x 6	x			
Knee support bandages	x	x		
Washing up liquid				x
Scourer/sponge				x
Camping table	x			
Camping odds & sods bag	x			
Deck chairs x 2				x
Sun cream	x			
Tripod for camcorder	x			
Road route cards	x			x
Train ticket	x			
Marker pen	x			
Fruit shoot bottles x 2	x			
Ordnance Survey maps	x			
Camcorder & tape	x			

RATIONS

ITEM	St & Ch	Al & Ve	Ma	Ge & Sue
Stew (cooked & frozen)	x			
Breakfast mix (sausage&bacon cooked, frozen & bagged)	x			
Beans (3 tins)	x			
Buttered rolls x 18		x		
Filled rolls (ham/coleslaw, cheese/ tomato, pork/stuffing x8 of each) labelled & wrapped seperately		x		
Bananas x 6				x
Pies/pasties x 10				x
Mixed nuts & raisins unsalted bagged x 4 bags		x		
Chocolate bars (fruit & nut) x 9		x		
Flapjack/muesli bars x 6				x
Unsweetened orange juice x 6 litres		x		

RESPONSIBILITIES(WHO WILL PROVIDE WHAT)

(St = Steve Ch = Chris Al = Alec Ve is Ve **Ma = Mark** Ge = Geoff Sue is Sue)

ITEM	St & Ch	Al & Ve	Ma	Ge & Sue
Custard pot x 2	X			
Tea bags	X			
Coffee	X			
Milk (1 pint carton)		X		
Carbo gel x 6	X			
Creatine tablets	X			
Salt	X			
Pepper	X			
Champagne	X			

FOR ON THE HILLS

	St & Ch	Al & Ve	Ma	Ge & Sue
Belly bag	X			
Day pack	X	X		
Bivvy bag	X	X		
Compass	X	X		
GPS	X			
Whistle	X	X		
Compeed	X			
First aid kit	X			
Route cards	X			
Waterproof (if rain forecast)	X	X		
Waterproof trousers (if torrential rain)	X	X		
Fleece	X	X		
Balaclava / hat (for Ben Nevis)	X	X		
Gloves (for Ben Nevis)	X	X		
Sandwich	X	X		
Platypus	X	X		
Camera	X	X		
Re-sealable plastic bags	X			
Extras for first aid kits.	X			
Small water bottles x 2	X			
Wine carrier bags (for sorting gear)	X			
Personal walking gear: walking poles, gaiters etc	X	X		

SUGGESTED FILMING PLAN

(Overall responsibility for filming rests with Mark Gibson.)

Film shot	Person
Arrival by Steve at Geoff's place	Chris
Preparations for departure	Chris
Film departure and goodbyes	Mark
Film arrival in **Dumfries**	Steve
Film final preparations & departure	Mark
Film scenery en route (A74; **Erskine Bridge**; **Loch Lomond**; **Rannoch Moor**;**Glen Coe** (stop at pass); **Buachaille**; **Ballachulish Bridge**; **Loch Linnhe**)	Steve
Arrival in **Fort William**, arrival at **Achintee** and film **Ben Nevis**	Steve
Warm up exercises, kitting up & final preparation	Mark
Departure for **Ben Nevis**	Mark
Film some of drivers' activities	Mark/Geoff
Film walkers return, getting into car, sorting selves out	Mark
Film part of journey in the dark, leaving **Fort William**, **Glen Coe**, **Glasgow**, stop at services, **Carlisle** etc.	Mark
Film walkers' preparations in car	Mark
Arrival in **Wasdale**	Steve
Walkers' departure for **Scafell Pike**	Mark
Film some of drivers' activities in middle of night	Mark/Geoff
Walkers return to car	Mark
Film Alec & Steve trying to sleep!	Mark/Geoff
Film part of journey to motorway	Mark/Geoff
Film getting close to **Snowdon**, first sighting of mountain	Steve
Film arrival at **Pen Y Pass**, & shots of **Snowdon**	Mark
Film drivers messing about	Mark/Geoff
Film walkers triumphant return & celebrations (Camera on tripod so all can be included)	Mark
Film part of journey to hotel and arrival there	Mark
Film part of final dinner	Steve
End credits	Steve

Steve to provide **'The End'** card and credits.

Annex 2

Datum OSGB, Position Format BNG (British National Grid)

Waypoint files in gpx file format are available for download from
DWG website www.walking.demon.co.uk/phfs.htm

BEN NEVIS

Wp	Easting		Northing	Description
1	NN 12604		72945	Gate at end of car park
2	NN 12589		72856	Turn left at signpost
3	NN 12836		72522	Stile
4	NN 13352		71998	Zigzag after youth hostel path
5	NN 13959		71808	Final metal bridge
6	NN 14104		71804	Veer left
7	NN 14348		72081	Zigzag left, then right
8	NN 14266		72112	Trend right
9	NN 14815		72302	Cross Red Burn, turn right
10	NN 14753		71854	Ford stream
11	NN 14701		71515	Zigzag left
12	NN 14939		71701	Zigzag right
13	NN 15139		71311	Zigzag left
14	NN 15269		71566	Zigzag right
15	NN 15307		71351	Zigzag left
16	NN 15530		71546	Zigzag right
17	NN 15582		71397	Zigzag left
18	NN 15702		71451	Zigzag right
19	NN 15724		71365	Turn 90° left (don't go straight)
20	NN 16171		71266	Gully on left
21	NN 16552		71197	Gardyloo Gully, turn left for summit
22	NN 16666		71277	Summit

SCAFELL PIKE

Datum OSGB, Position Format BNG (British National Grid)

Waypoint files in gpx file format are available for download from
DWG website www.walking.demon.co.uk/phfs.htm

Wp	Easting	Northing	Description
1	NY 18074	07612	Start - campsite lane end
2	NY 18325	07385	Bridge
3	NY 18634	07219	Turn left over footbridge
4	NY 18652	07236	Turn right after footbridge
5	NY 18730	07244	Gate
6	NY 19228	07309	Gate 2
7	NY 19517	07447	Ford, turn right over gill
8	NY 20090	07313	Cairn
9	NY 20217	07326	Fork in path, go left
10	NY 20701	07471	Start of zigzags
11	NY 21061	07712	Turn right for summit
12	NY 21145	07540	Veer right up crags
13	NY 21496	07272	Turn right up to summit
14	NY 21542	07210	Summit

SNOWDON - PYG TRACK

Datum OSGB, Position Format BNG (British National Grid)

Waypoint files in gpx file format are available for download from
DWG website www.walking.demon.co.uk/phfs.htm

Wp	Easting	Northing	Description
1	SH 64736	55606	Pen y Pass car park
2	SH 64342	55503	Rocky outcrops to left
3	SH 63847	55365	Veer right
4	SH 63457	55400	Turn left
5	SH 63342	54851	Double stile at Bwlch y Moch
6	SH 61510	54866	Junction with Miners' Track
7	SH 61005	54830	Start of zigzags
8	SH 60775	54854	Pigtop Pillar
9	SH 60969	54368	Summit

SNOWDON - MINERS' TRACK

Datum OSGB, Position Format BNG (British National Grid)

Waypoint files in gpx file format are available for download from
DWG website www.walking.demon.co.uk/phfs.htm

Wp	Easting	Northing	Description
1	SH 64744	55631	Pen y Pass car park
2	SH 64668	54873	Right hand bend
3	SH 63476	54555	Turn right for causeway
4	SH 63322	54872	End of causeway, turn left
5	SH 61966	54721	Glaslyn
6	SH 61698	54850	Leave Glaslyn, steep climb
7	SH 61425	54844	Junction with Pyg Track
8	SH 61022	54844	Zigzag
9	SH 60771	54823	Pigtop Pillar
10	SH 60969	54368	Summit

SNOWDON - PYG TRACK ASCENT, MINERS' TRACK DESCENT

Datum OSGB, Position Format BNG (British National Grid)

Waypoint files in gpx file format are available for download from
DWG website www.walking.demon.co.uk/phfs.htm

Wp	Easting	Northing

Wps 1 to 9 same as Pyg Track waypoints then:-

Wp	Easting	Northing
10	SH60771	54823
11	SH61425	54834
12	SH61698	54721
13	SH61966	54577
14	SH63322	54872
15	SH63476	54555
16	SH64668	54873
17	SH64744	55631

Annex 3 ACCOMMODATION LIST

BEN NEVIS

The Ben Nevis Inn (bunkhouse accommodation) 01397 701227
www.ben-nevis-inn.co.uk*

Woodside B&B, Fort William 01397 705897
www.woodsidefortwilliam.co.uk

Glen Nevis Youth Hostel 01397 702336 www.glennevishostel.co.uk*

Glen Nevis Campsite 01397 702191 www.glen-nevis.co.uk

Bank Street Lodge 01397 700070 www.bankstreetlodge.co.uk

SCAFELL PIKE

The Wasdale Head Inn 019467 26229 www.wasdale.com*

Burnthwaite Farm B&B, Wasdale Head 019467 26229
www.burnthwaitefarm.co.uk*

Wasdale Head National Trust Campsite 019467 26229
www.nationaltrust.org.uk*

Borrowdale Youth Hostel 0870 770 5706 www.yha.org.uk*

Scafell Hotel, Rosthwaite 017687 77208 www.scafell.co.uk

SNOWDON

Cobdens Hotel, Capel Curig 01690 720243 www.cobdens.co.uk*

Pen y Gwyrd Hotel 01286 870211 www.pyg.co.uk

Pen y Pass Youth Hostel 0870 770 5990 www.yha.org.uk*

Beech Bank B & B, Llanberis 01286 871085 www.beech-bank.co.uk

Snowdon House Bunkhouse 01286 870284
www.snowdonhouse.co.uk

Camping in Llanberis 01286 870923 www.campinginllanberis.com

*With the exception of those premises marked with an asterisk – where
we have personally stayed - inclusion in this list should not be taken as
a recommendation.*

GPS The Easy Way
by David Brawn
(Discovery Walking Guides 2nd edition 2006 ISBN 9781904946229
£4.99)

The Yorkshire Three Peaks Challenge
by Paul Shorrock
(Discovery Walking Guides 2010 ISBN 9781904946649 £4.99)

A Walk in the Woods
by Bill Bryson
(Black Swan 1997 ISBN 9780552997027 £8.99)

Down Under
by Bill Bryson (Black Swan 2001 ISBN 9780552997034 £8.99)

Notes from a Small Island
by Bill Bryson (Black Swan 1996 ISBN 9780552996006 £8.99)

Wild Trails to Far Horizons
by Mike Cudahy
(Hayloft Publishing 1989 ISBN 9781904524700 £17.99 and Daily
Telegraph, 7 August 2009)

McCarthy's Bar: A Journey of Discovery in Ireland
by Pete McCarthy
(Sceptre 2001 ISBN 9780340766057 £8.99)

Mersey Venture Three Peaks Challenge
http://users.tinyonline.co.uk/richieev/tp

Three Peaks, Ten Tors
by Ronald Turnbull
(Cicerone Press 2007 ISBN 9781852845018 £14.00)

**The Southern Fells Second Edition (Pictorial Guides to the
Lakeland Fells)**
by Alfred Wainwright
(Frances Lincoln 2007 ISBN 9780711226586 £13.99)

Wasdale Mountain Rescue Team Report
www.mountain.rescue.org.uk/news 2007

Guy Newbold www.outdoorsmagic.com/news 2002

by David Brawn

Making a successful Challenge on the National 3 Peaks depends on three factors:-

FITNESS:- being fit enough to complete the three mountain walking sections fast enough,

LOGISTICS:- organising yourself and your team to be in the right place with the right equipment and ready to go at the right time,

NAVIGATION:- getting from your start point up to the top of the three peaks and down again and driving between the peaks, without getting lost or delayed.

Getting 'two out of three' factors correct is not an option as this will doom you to failure. In Steve's account of his and Alec's successful challenge, you'll notice several opportunities for failure, including 'stopping for a meal because you are ahead of time', '62mph limited minibus instead of a 70mph car' and 'getting lost on the mountain'.

IMPORTANCE OF ACCURATE NAVIGATION

Steve and Alec invested a lot of time in training and researching their routes, both mountain walking and driving, before tackling the Challenge proper. Even their thoroughly prepared Challenge attempt held little allowance for the unexpected. Their planned time was 23 hours 30 minutes, while their actual time of 22 hours 29 minutes allowed preciously little time for errors. Just one wrong turn (see the 'TomTom incident') on the driving stages or any of the three mountains could have had them slipping into failure despite all their training and preparation.

Accurate navigation is vital if you are to succeed on the challenge; so important that you should include the methodology into your planning from the start. Whatever you might think of traditional 'Map & Compass' navigation, GPS is the most accurate navigation system on the mountain, dependent upon having good reception. Remember you will have one night mountain walking route where if you go wrong you could not only fail the Challenge but risk physical danger. Finding your way back onto the correct route at night after a navigational error is both difficult and time consuming.

GPS NAVIGATION

GPS units give an accuracy of approx 5 metres on the 3 Peaks walking routes when you have good satellite reception, which will be almost all of the time depending upon the configuration of satellites at the time you are walking. Steve's waypoints (in Annex 2) can be loaded into your GPS unit memory and called up for each walking route; you could also load all the waypoints as one file in memory. These waypoints will tell you when you are reaching the points described in Steve's descriptions. It's most reassuring to know exactly where you are and that you are on the correct route. Steve's waypoints are available to download from the DWG website at www.walking.demon.co.uk/pnfs.htm in gpx file format which are compatible with a wide range of GPS software.

GPS will provide you with the 'pinpoint' navigational accuracy that could be all important to the success of your Challenge, but you would be well advised to:-:

● familiarise yourself with GPS through a book such as 'GPS The Easy Way' or 'GPS for Walkers' and
● use your GPS (and software) regularly so that you become familiar with its use and accuracy.

Once you get into regular use you'll find your GPS does much more than just tell you where you are as it records where you have been and with preloaded Tracks and Waypoints can show you where you want to go.

GPS will provide you with a detailed record of your '3 Peaks' training; most importantly, you can record your training ascents and descents on the 3 Peaks themselves. By recording the three successful training ascents and descents of Ben Nevis, Scafell Pike and Snowdon, your GPS will give you valuable information. Your GPS record will show you exactly where you have walked (your GPS track) and you can record all the important points along your route, e.g. decision points such as which path to take at junctions, as waypoints. Now you will have records of your successful ascents and descents of each peak that you can now load into your GPS ,to use during the actual 24 hours of your challenge.

GPS & SAT-NAV EQUIPMENT

Mapping GPS units show your position against a detailed background map such as OS Landranger 50k scale maps and OS Explorer 25k scale digital mapping is available for most mapping GPS units. These units give you real time mapping with a moving map display using the OS maps you are familiar with. Seeing exactly where you are on the map really is a revelation in outdoor navigation. Once you have used one of these mapping GPS units you are very unlikely to go back to a basic GPS unit for your adventuring.

We have 'trail tested' the Adventurer 3500 from Memory Map and the Lowrance Endura from Mapyx Quo and can recommend both these units. Other manufacturers of mapping GPS units include SatMap, Garmin, TwoNav and Magellan.

Equipment doesn't have to be expensive to give you 'pinpoint' navigational accuracy. GPS units range from the basic Garmin eTrex at around £80 with mapping GPS units ranging from £250 upwards to £500 depending upon the manufacturer and digital mapping package that come swith the unit. As with all battery powered equipment make sure you are carrying spare batteries with you.

MemoryMap produce a National Parks CD, including the 3 Peaks, for around £30. These are 'pocket money' prices compared to the time and expense you will put into your Challenge and a bargain if they assist in your success.

The key to GPS and Sat-Nav is to understand your equipment, use it regularly so you are familiar with its use, and in the case of Sat-Nav load the latest updates for your system.

Annex 5 EXPERTS AFTER THE EVENT

by David Brawn

Steve and Alec's Challenge was well planned, they trained hard, walked all three peaks before the actual event, they had a good support team - and they succeeded!

You can think of the Challenge as a twenty-four hour event. According to Steve and Alec's plan, they expected to finish in 23 hours 30 minutes, just a 2% margin of error; while their actual time of 22 hours 29 provides only a 6% margin of error. These are very small margins. When making your own Challenge, it will be important that you eliminate potential errors if you are to succeed. While it is easy to look like an expert with hindsight, here are some areas where I think I can add to Steve and Alec's experiences for the potential benefit of Challengers.

IS THE CHALLENGE IMPORTANT TO YOU?

Most readers will probably answer 'yes', but there are different degrees of 'yes'! Follow Steve's advice, especially on training and knowledge of the walking routes (navigation). The objective is to minimise the risk of failure so in addition to Steve's advice we'll add:-

WEEKEND THINKING

The weekend nearest to the Summer Equinox (the longest day) is when most Challengers make their attempt, resulting in crowded routes and the aggravation felt by Steve at the **Snowdon** 'Saturday amblers' while completing his Challenge. If you want nice clear routes free of human obstruction, then plan your Challenge for weekdays.

NIGHT WALKING IS LIKE DAY WALKING WITH A TORCH

Oh no it isn't. While you might be able to see the path immediately ahead, that's all you can see with a torch. My experience of night walking is traversing the Las Cañadas crater below Mount Teide (Tenerife) by the February 2007 Full Moon. Take my word for it, it's is nothing like walking the route by day.

You'll need to walk at least one mountain in the dark to succeed, so get some experience of night walking. While Steve and Alec chose the weekend closest to the longest day for maximum daylight, my choice would be the Full Moon nearest to the Summer Solstice for maximum moonlight on the night route. You don't appreciate how valuable the light is until you haven't got it!

I'M NOT USING THAT / THOSE

Don't rule out any equipment or options that could improve your chance of success; remember the margin for failure is very small, so every little helps. Walkers tend to be rather strong minded on walking matters, whether it be walking poles, GPS, clothing, equipment or really any matter to do with walking. Cast aside any prejudices you might have so that you can train with, and use on your Challenge, any equipment or option that could improve your chances of success.

WE'LL TAKE YOUR CAR

Twenty four hours might be a long time in politics and it's also a long time to be in a moving car, which is where you'll be for most of your Challenge. Deciding which vehicle to use in not a light decision of, 'We'll take your car.'

You need a vehicle that can cruise at the motorway speed limit, with enough space and comfort for yourselves and your drivers. It will need to be reliable as even a small mishap could cost you dearly; remember that small margin between success and failure.

If you are using one of your team's vehicles, it's a good idea to have it serviced and checked shortly before your planned Challenge. No suitable vehicle? Then look at hiring what you need, but do check the regulations - remember those 62mph minibuses.

So, assuming you will be following Steve's advice based on his successful Challenge with Alec, it only remains for me to wish you the best of luck.

David Brawn
Discovery Walking Guides Ltd & Instant-Books UK Ltd